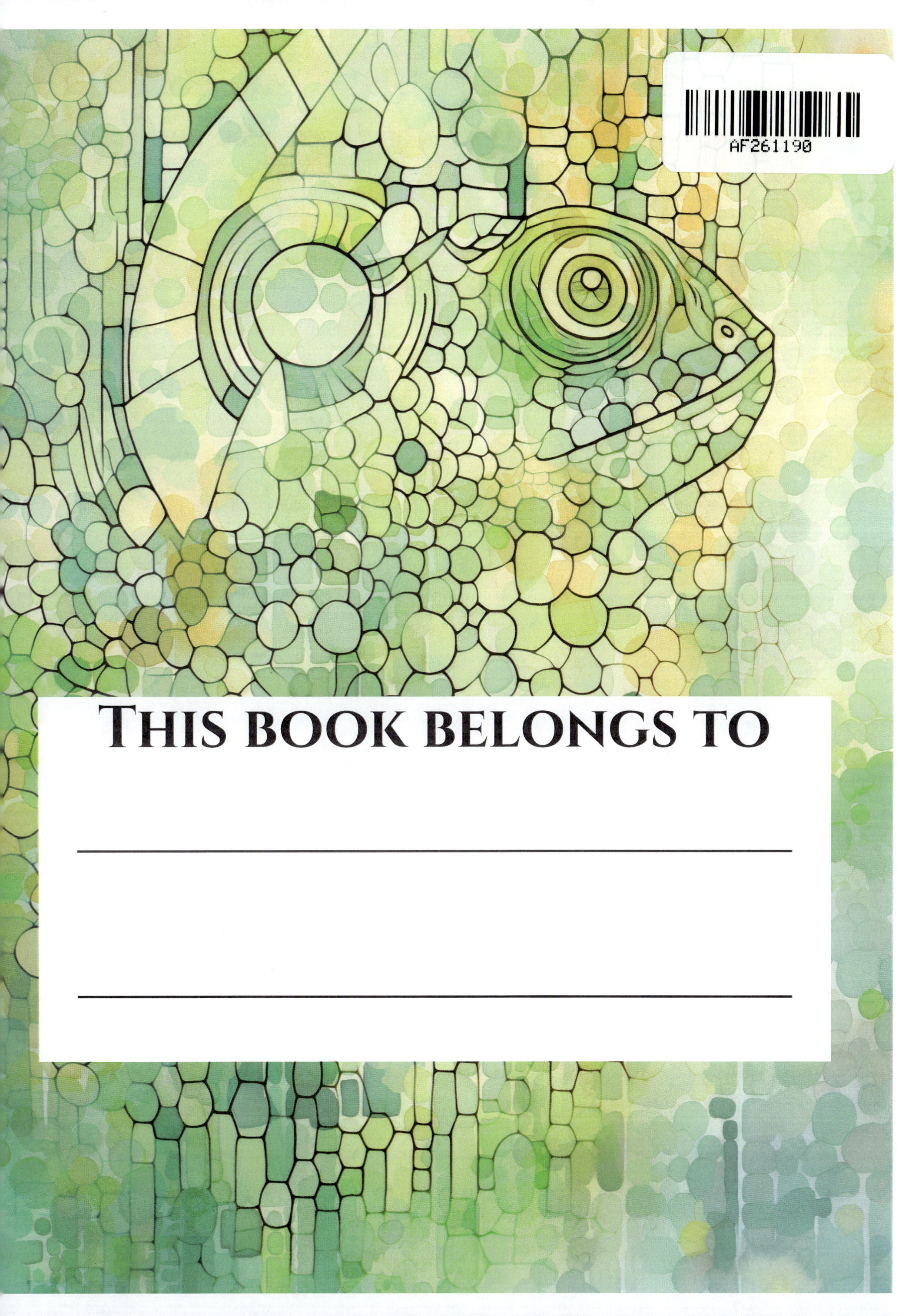
AF261190
THIS BOOK BELONGS TO

Intentionally left blank

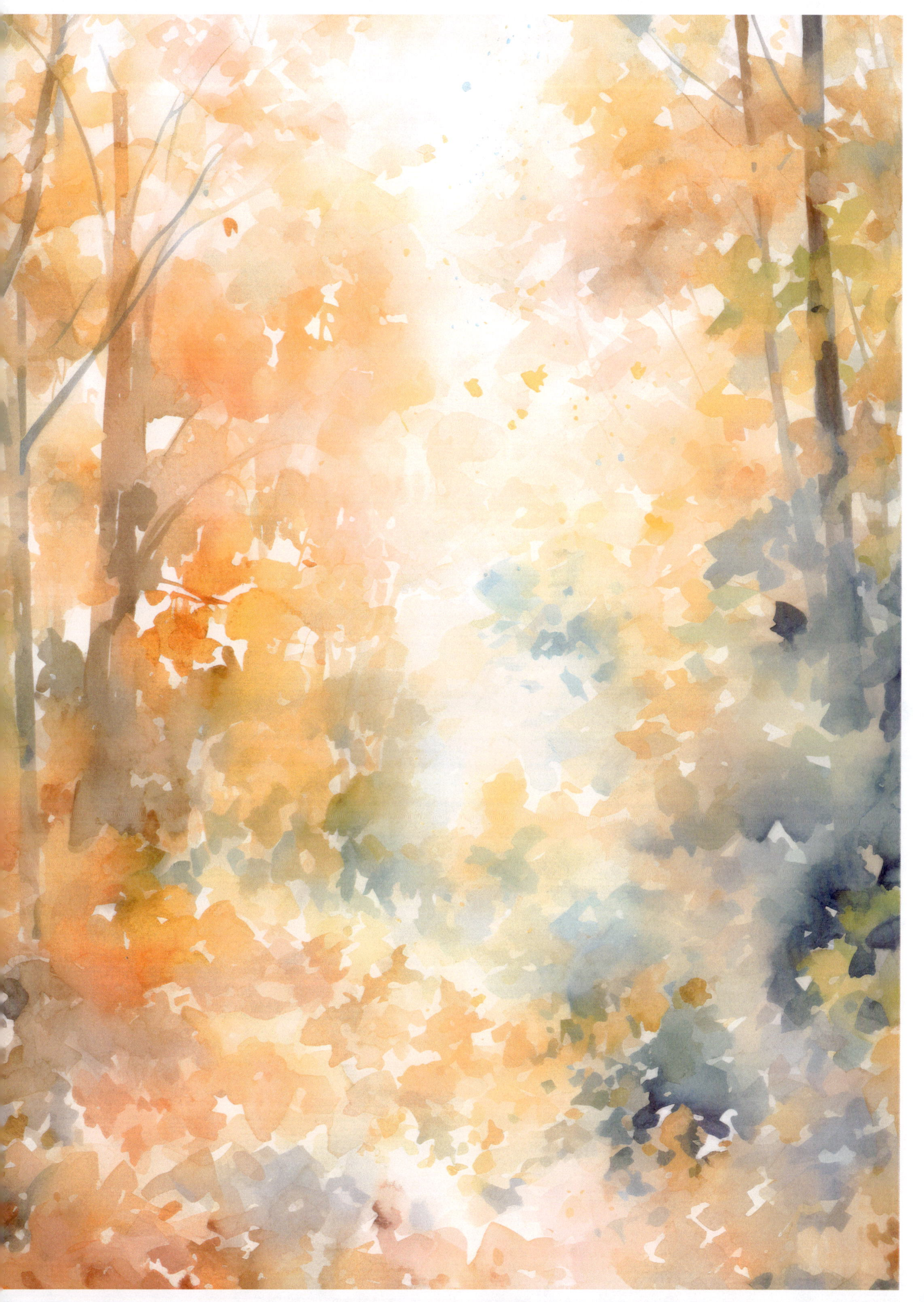

Intentionally left blank

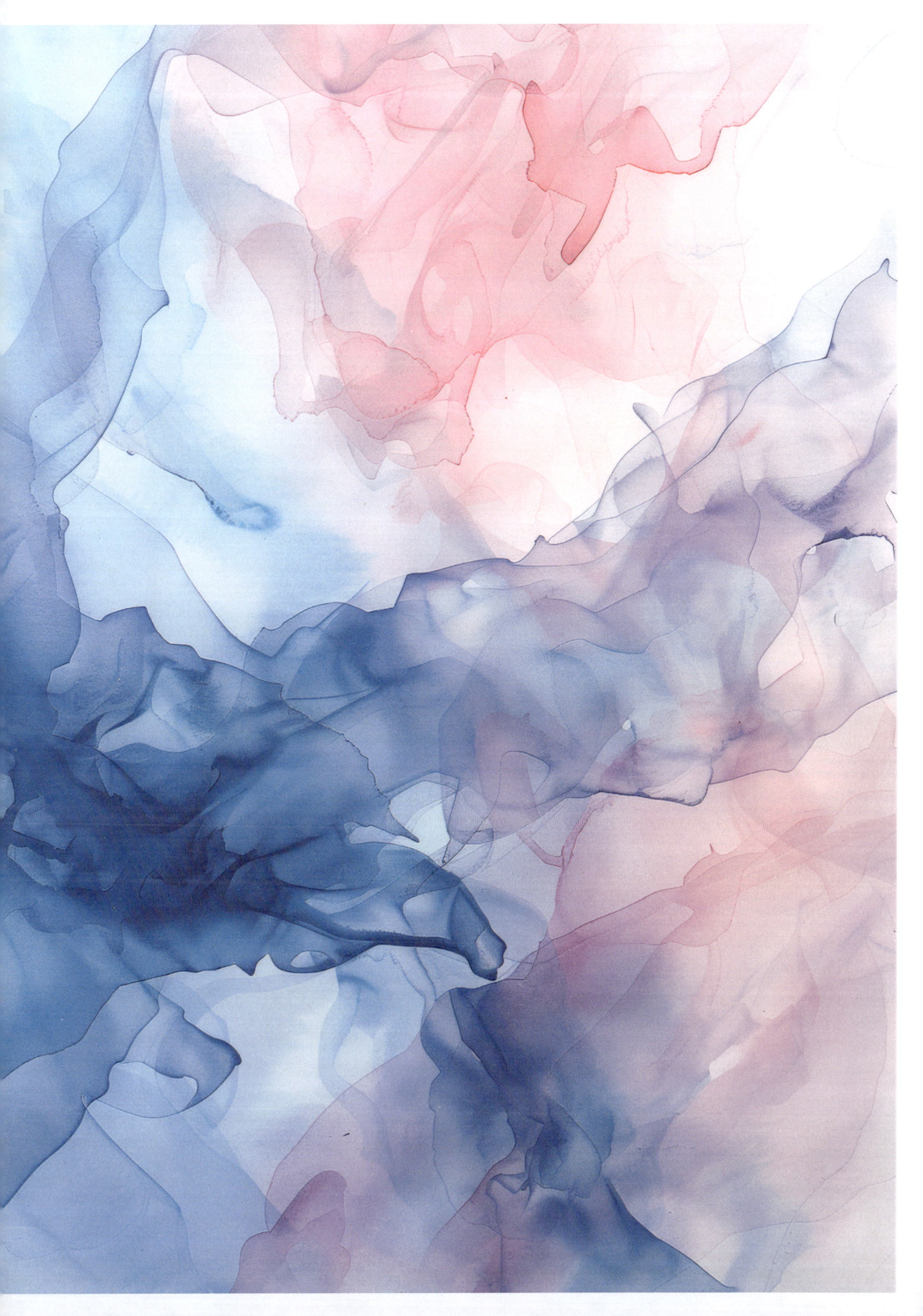

Intentionally left blank

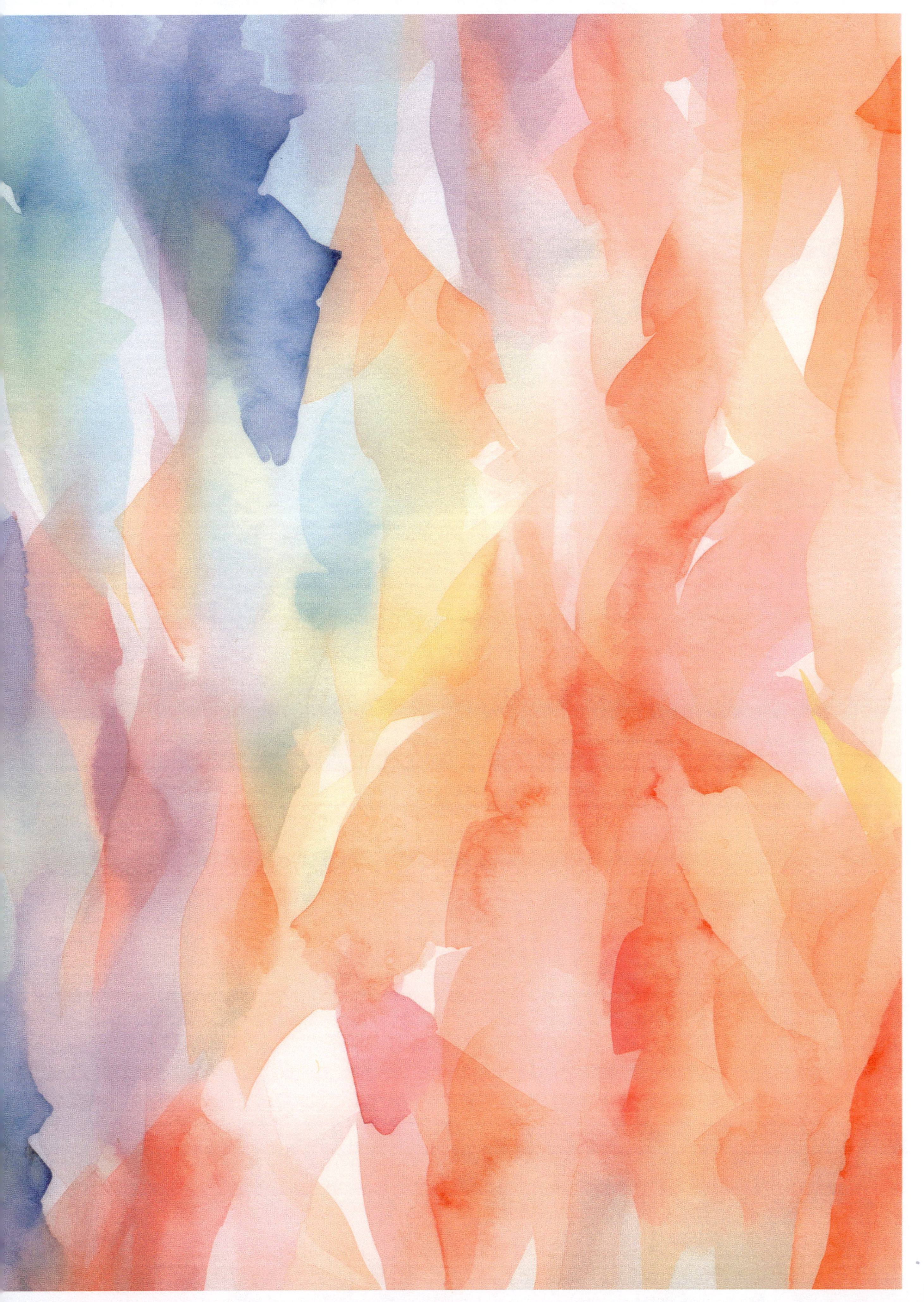

Intentionally left blank

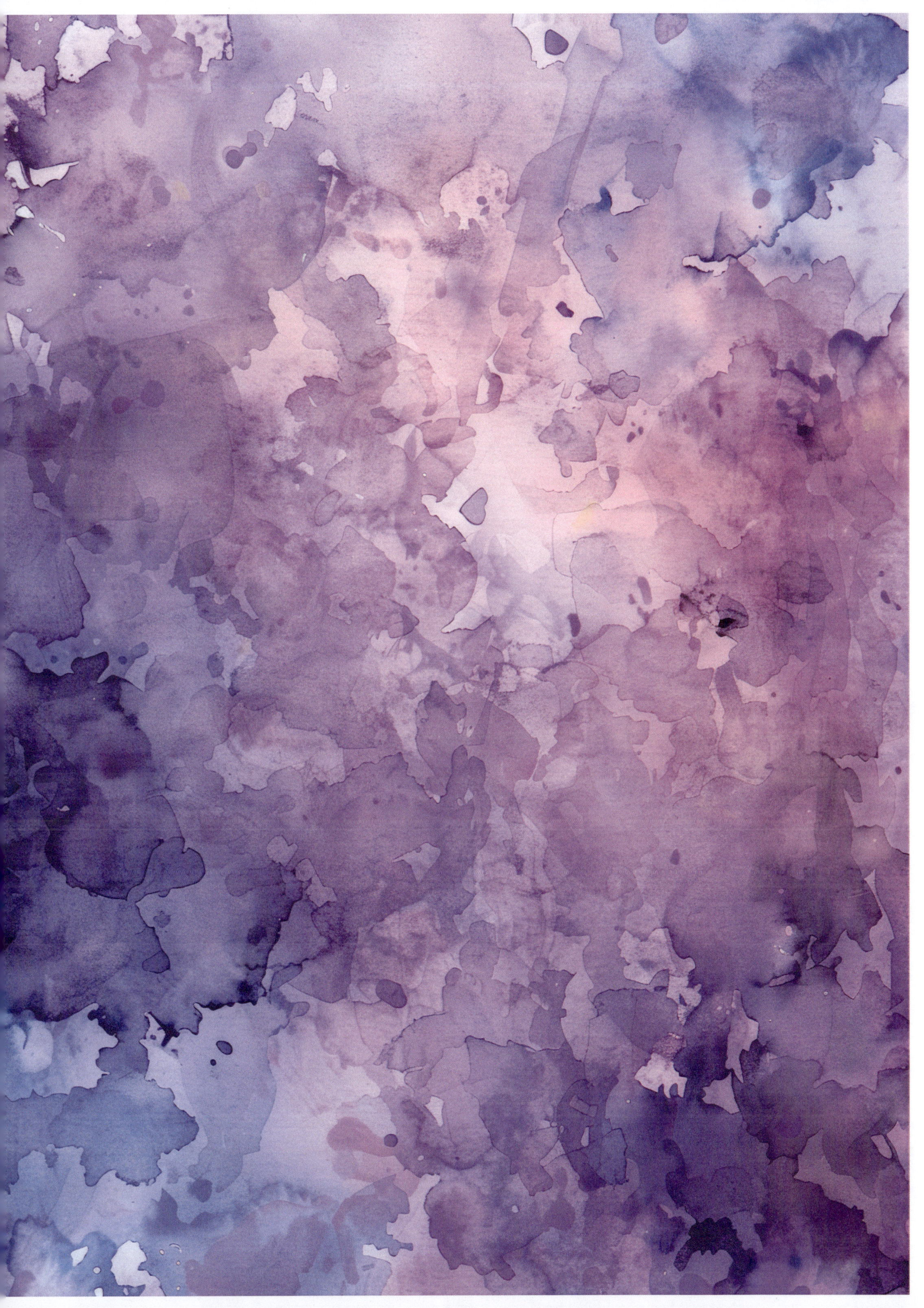

Intentionally left blank

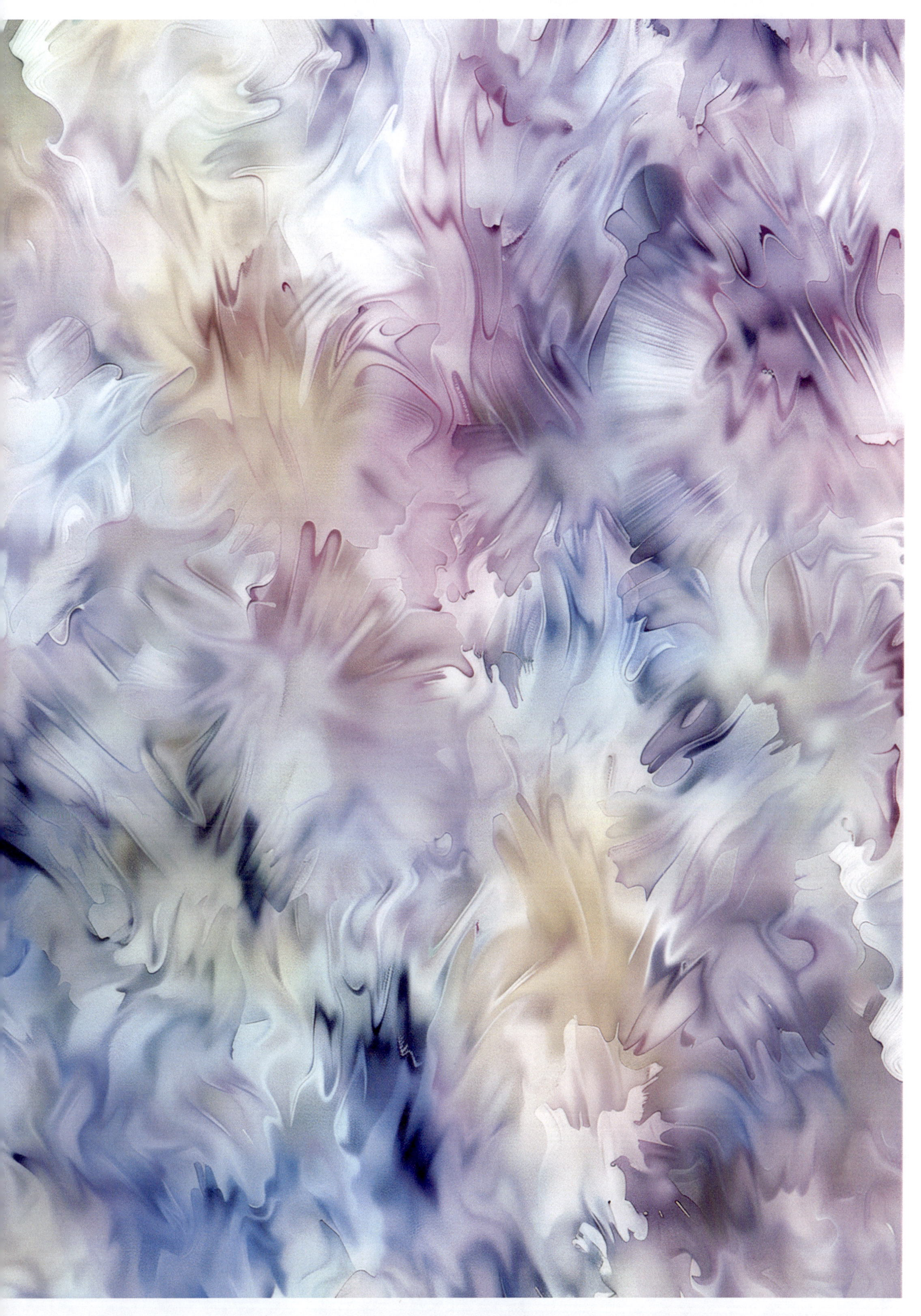

Intentionally left blank

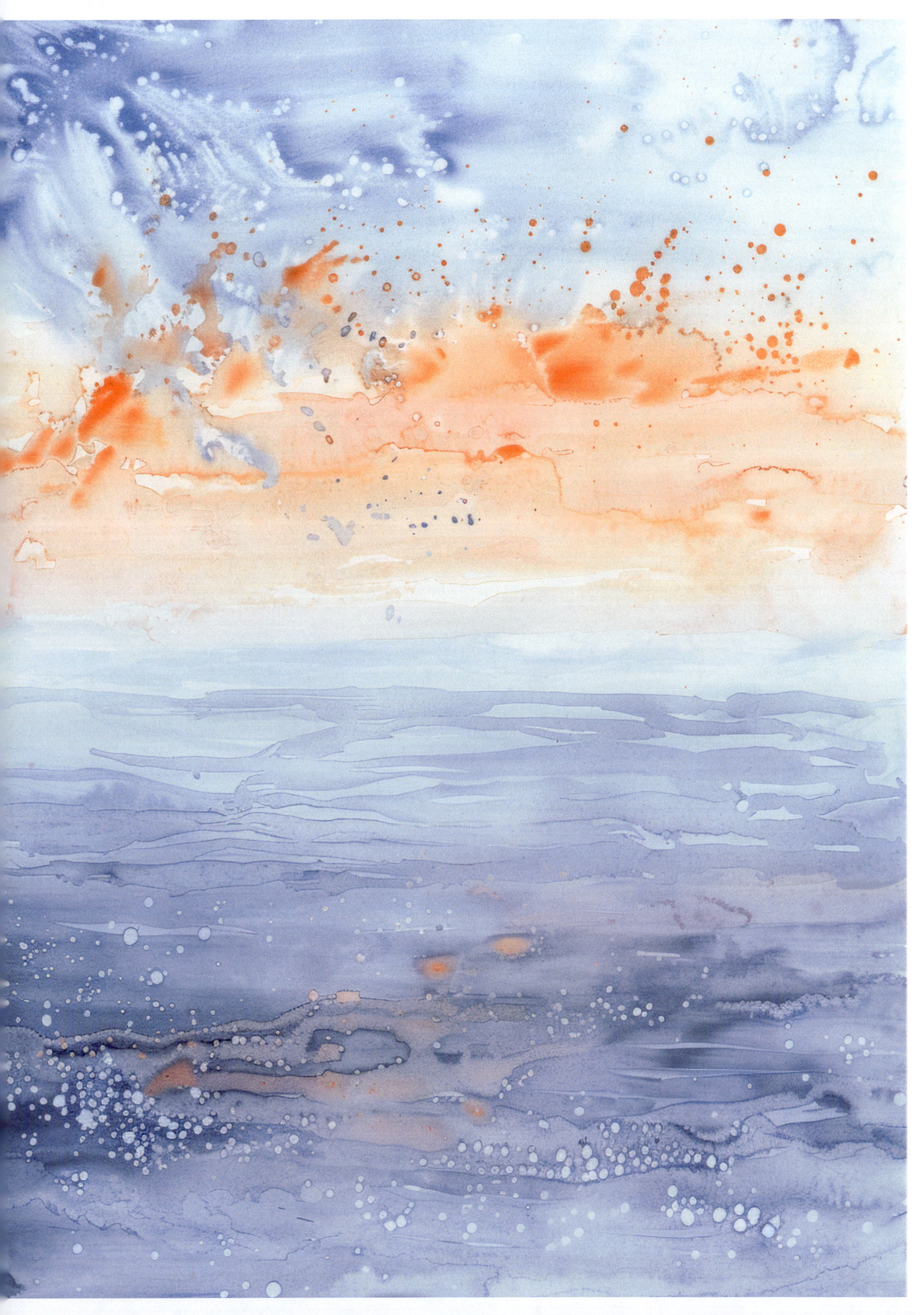

Intentionally left blank

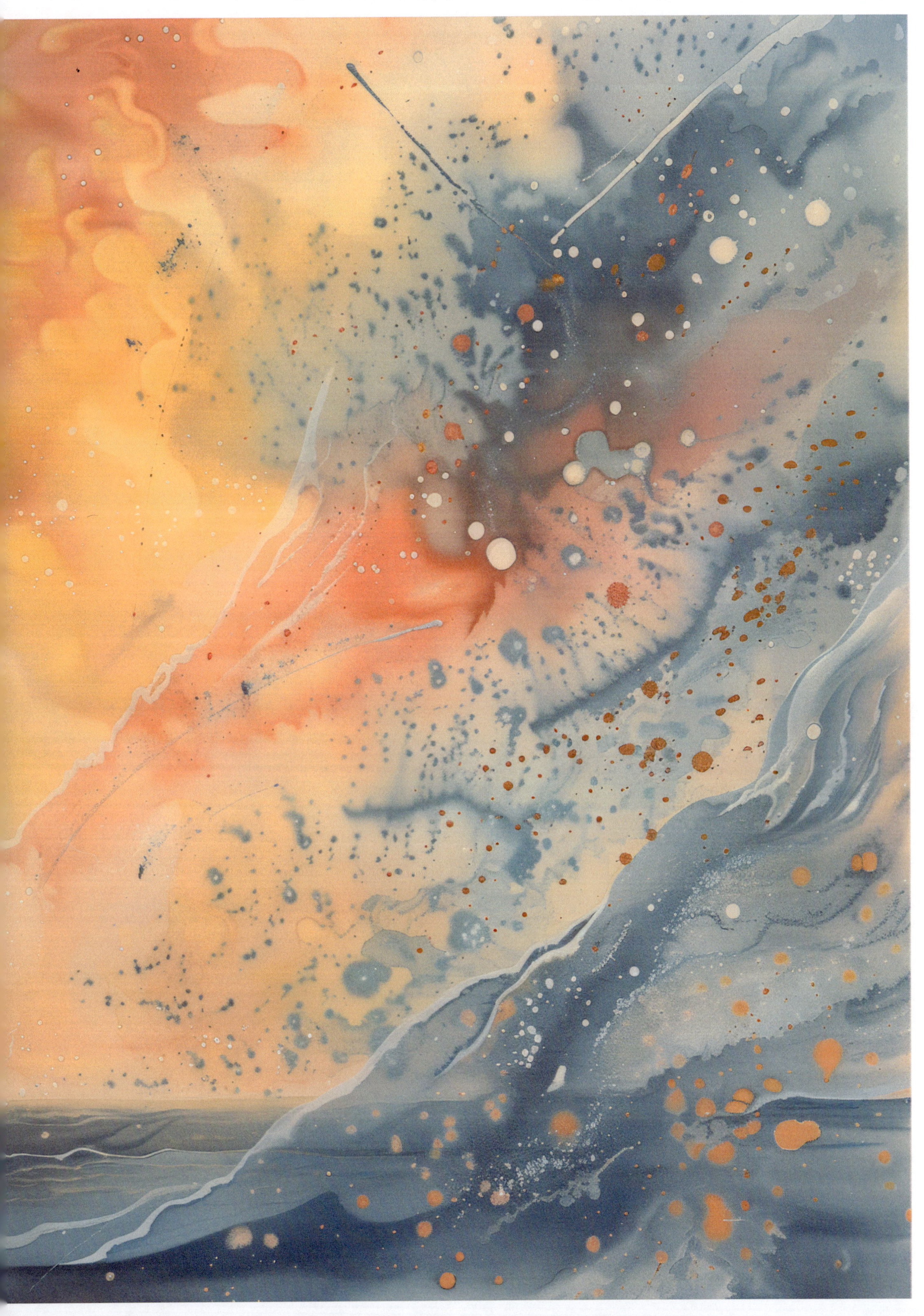

Intentionally left blank

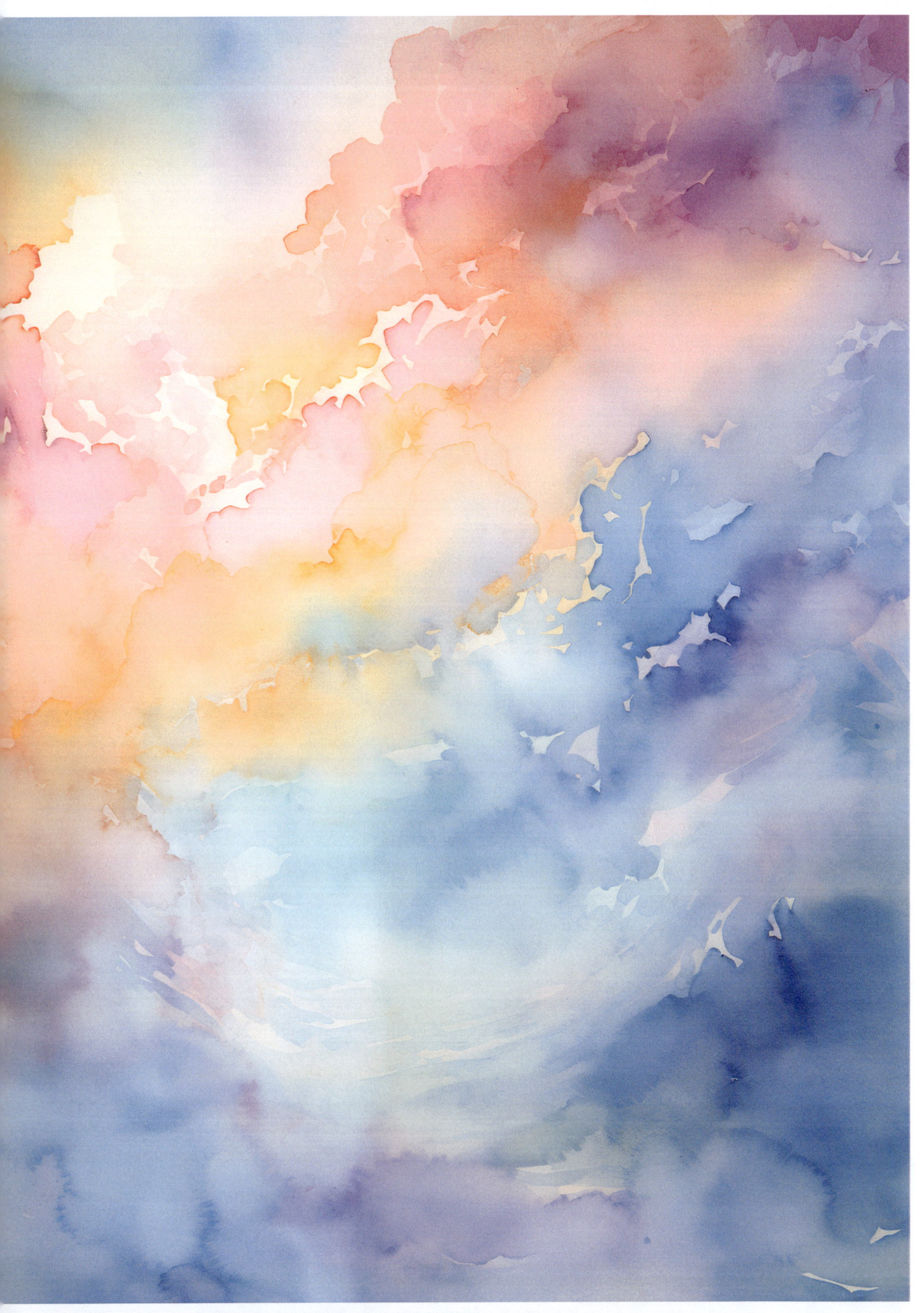

Intentionally left blank

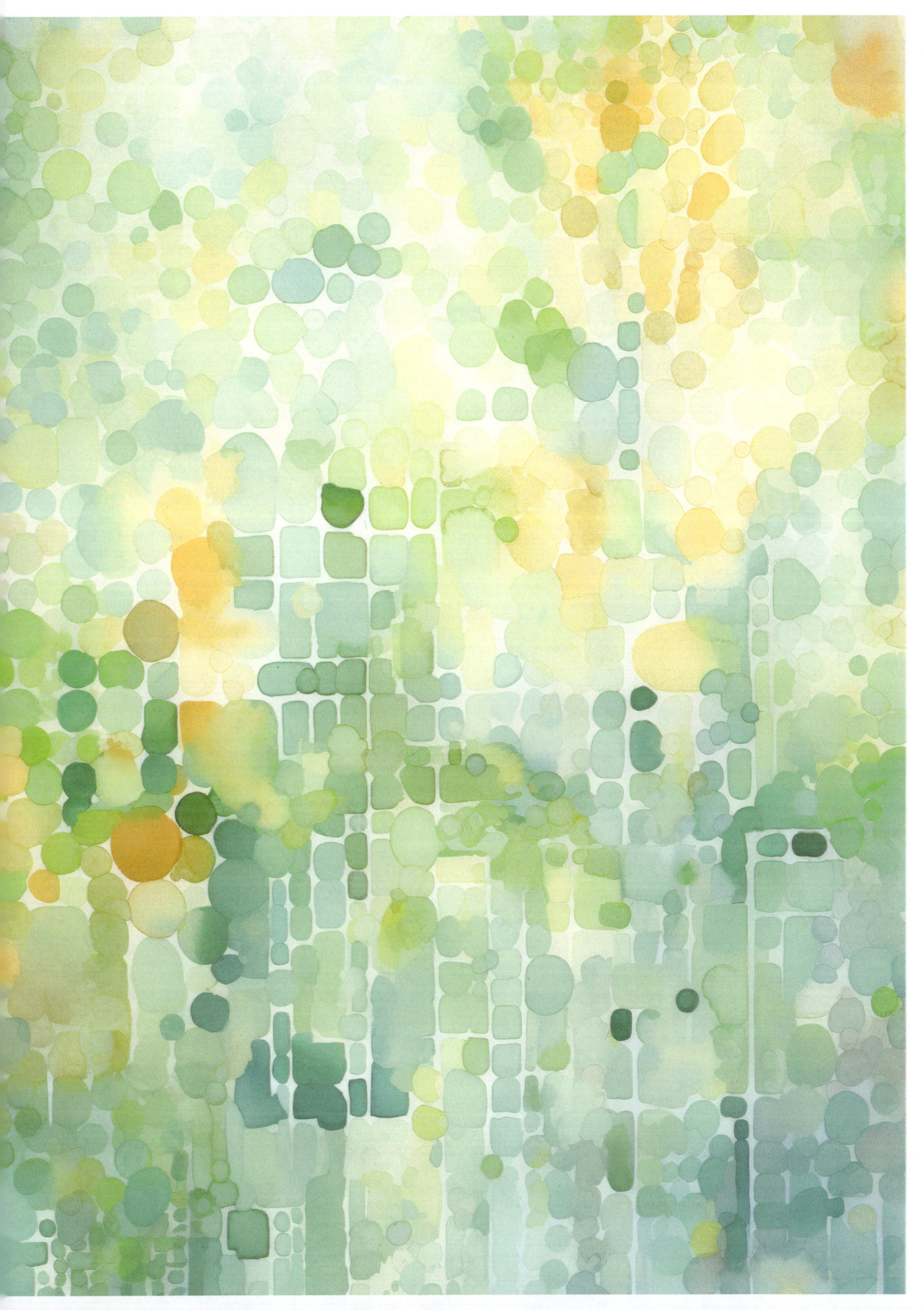

Intentionally left blank

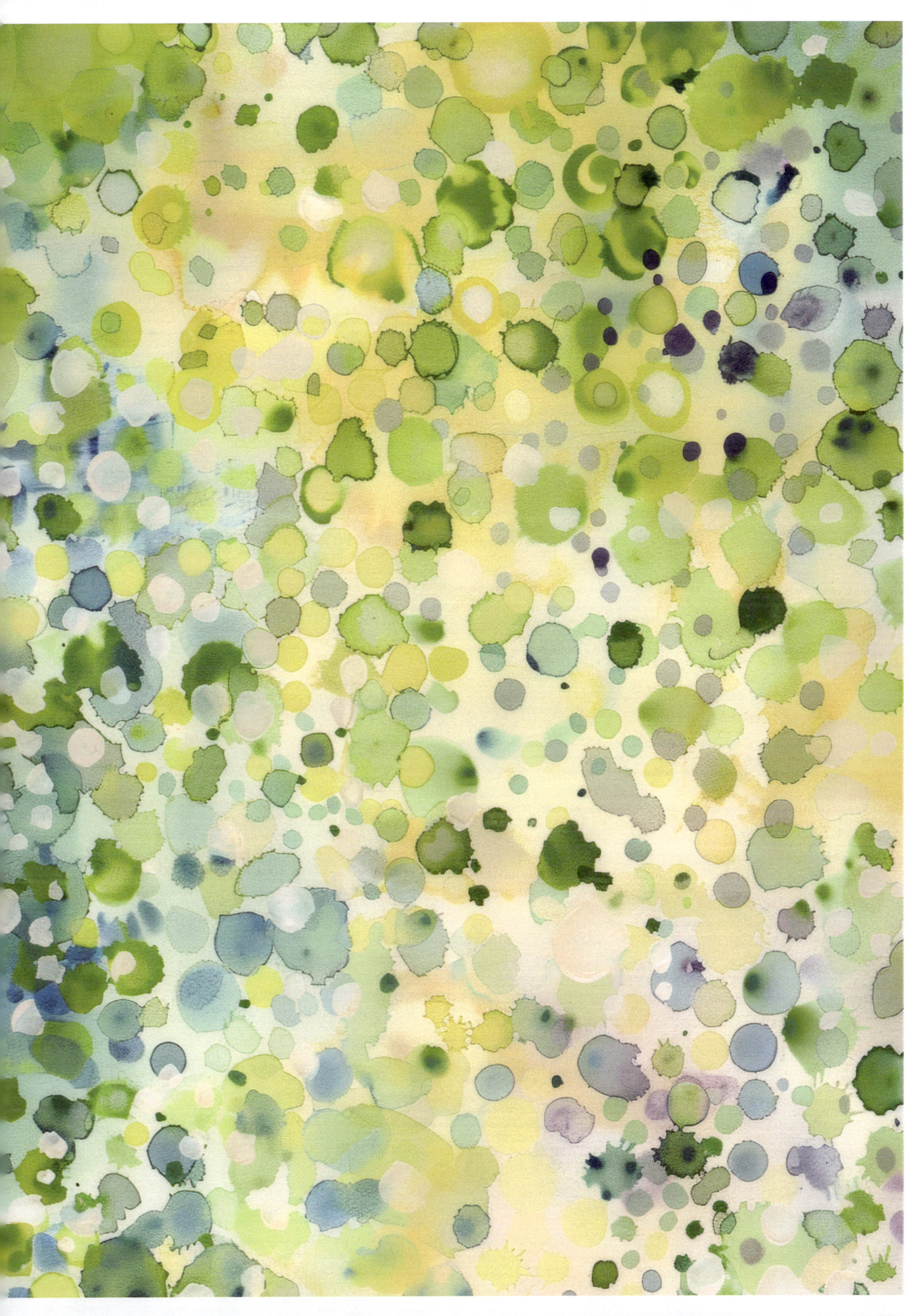

Intentionally left blank

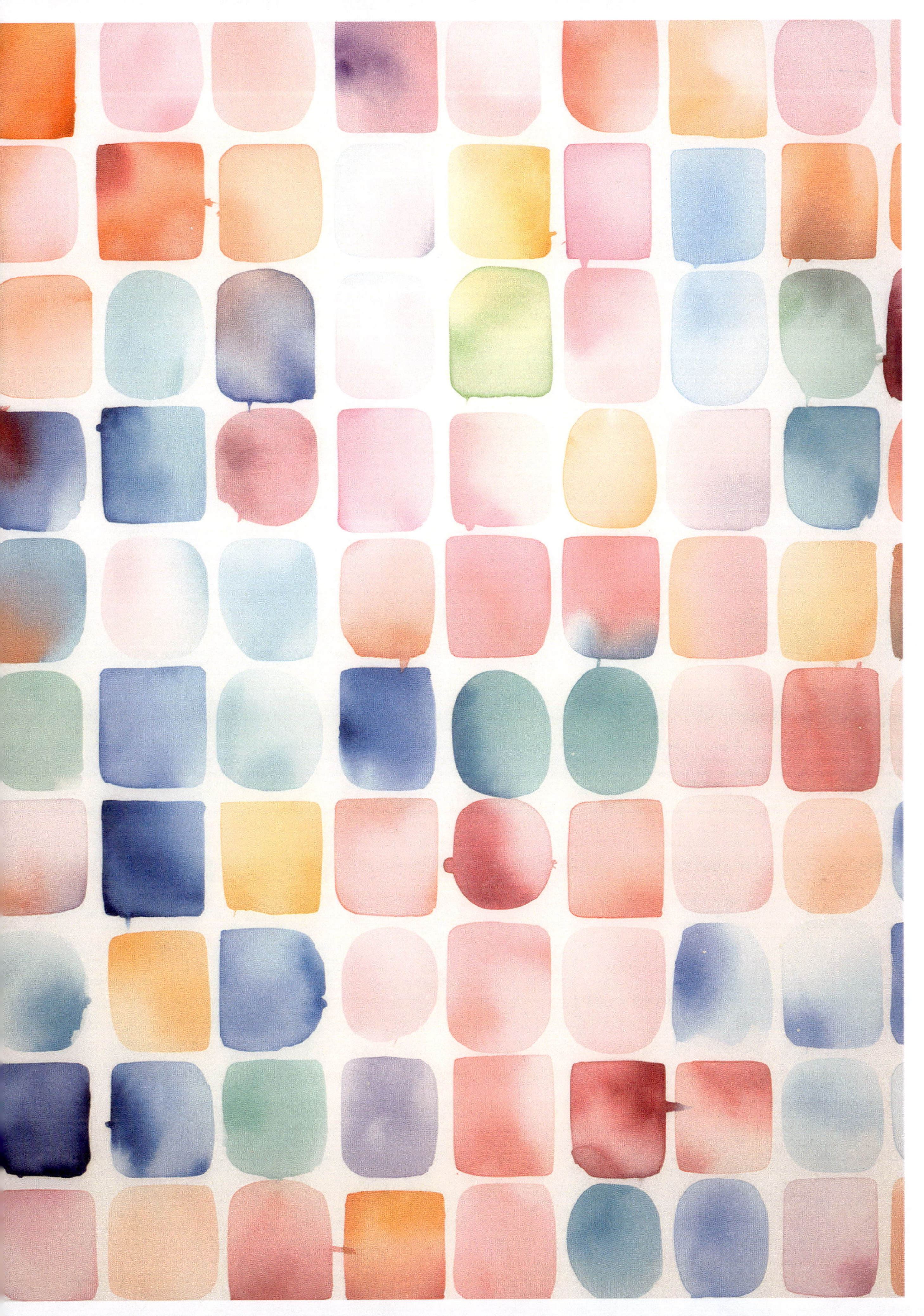

Intentionally left blank

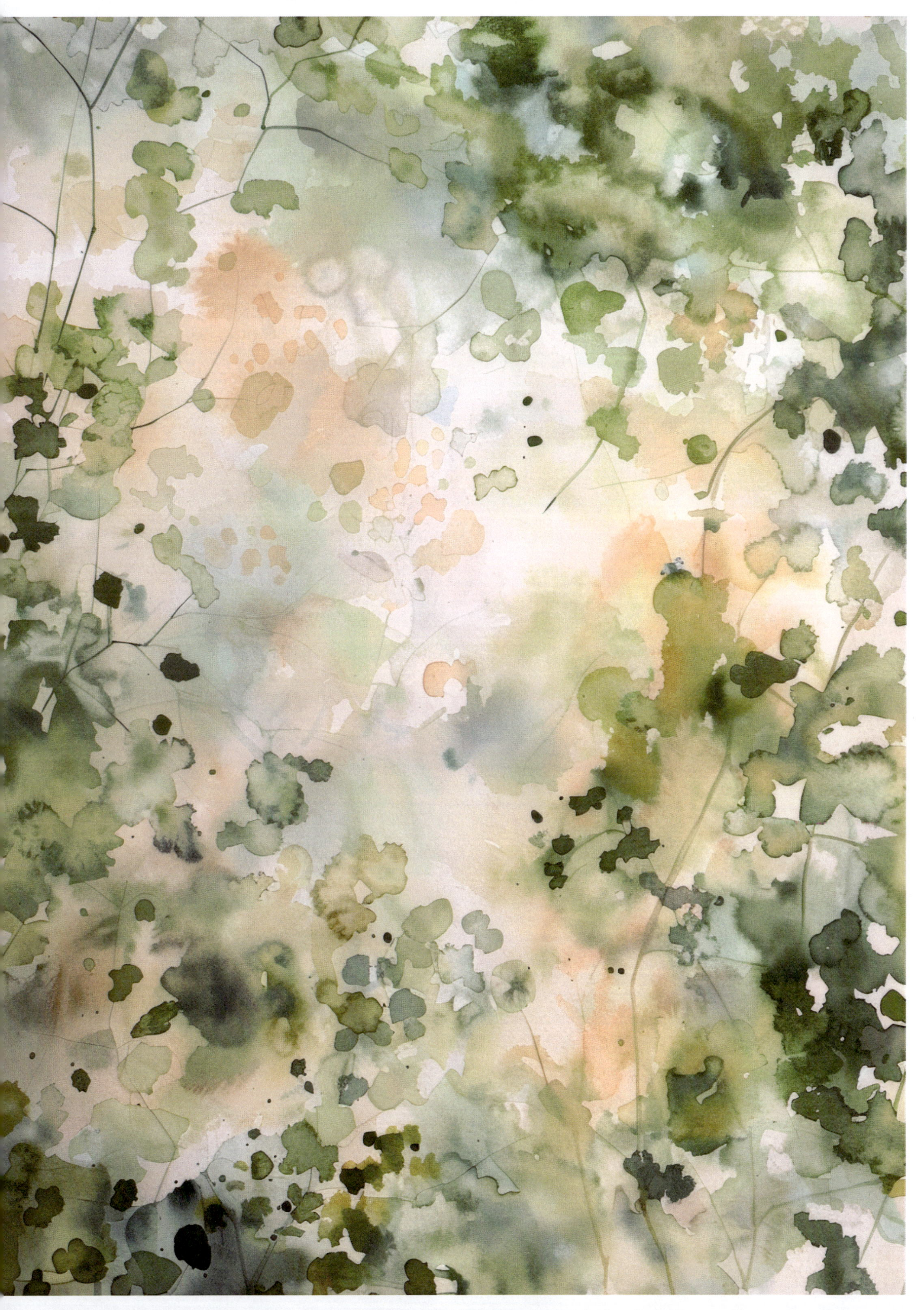

Intentionally left blank

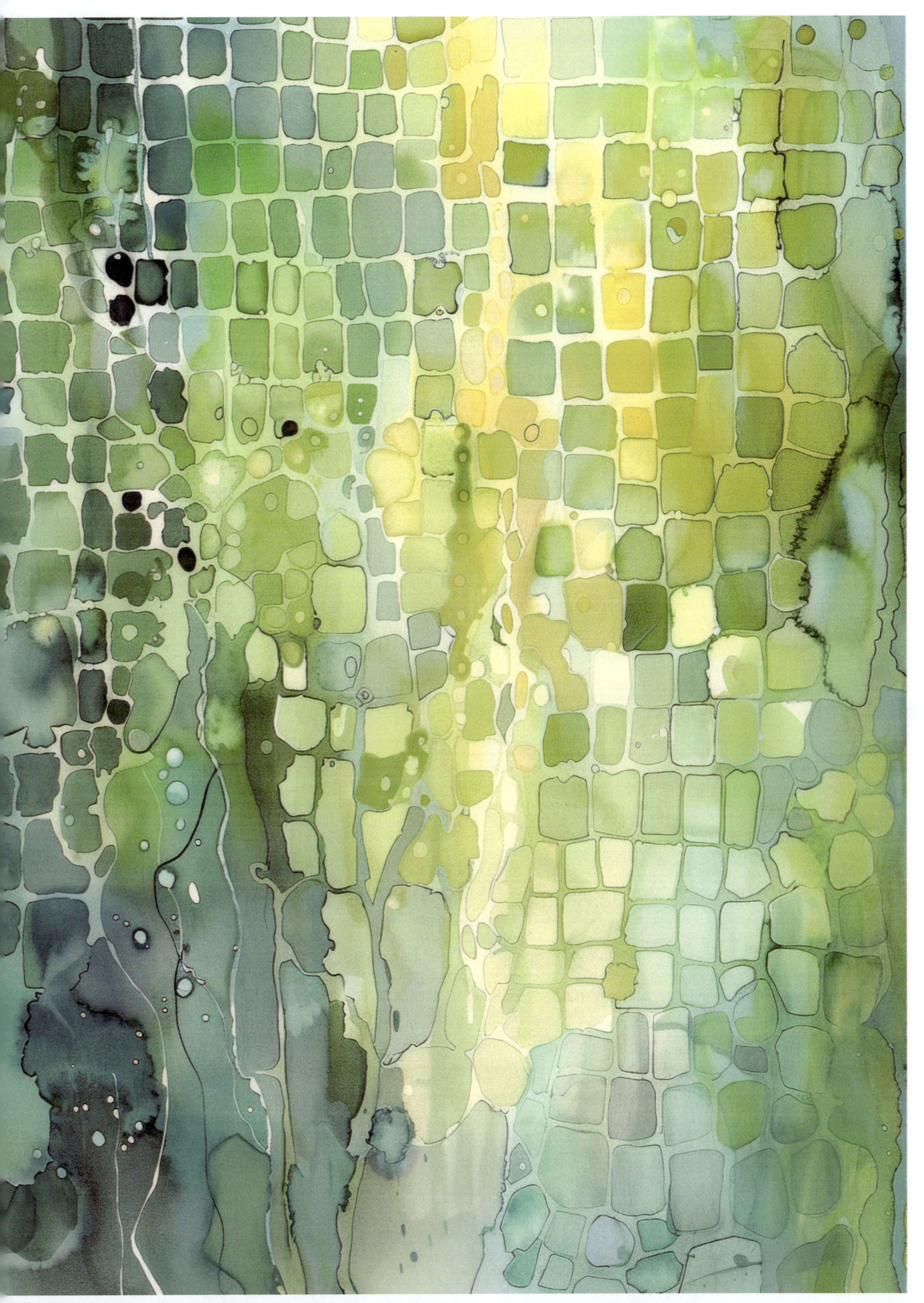

Intentionally left blank

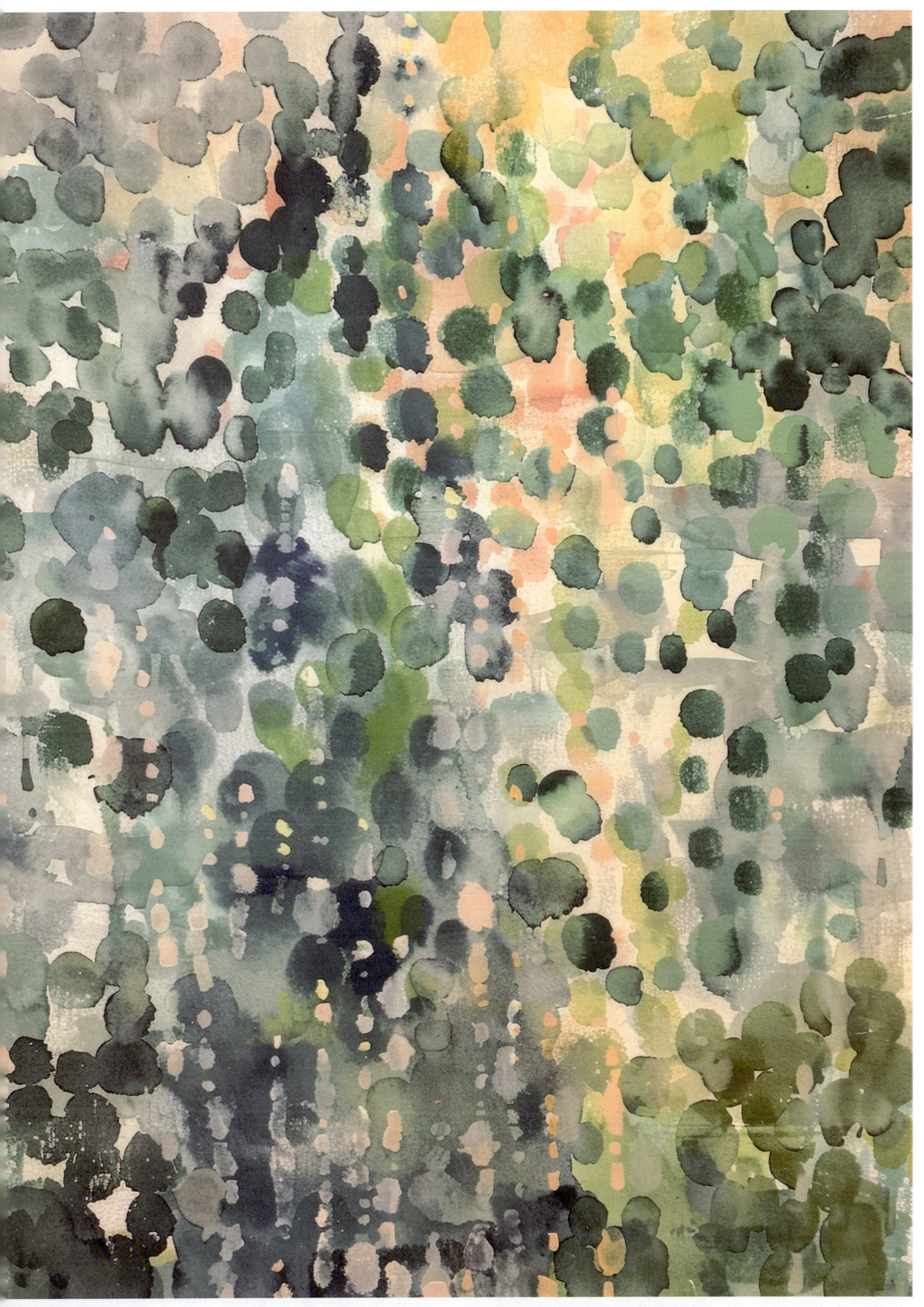

Intentionally left blank

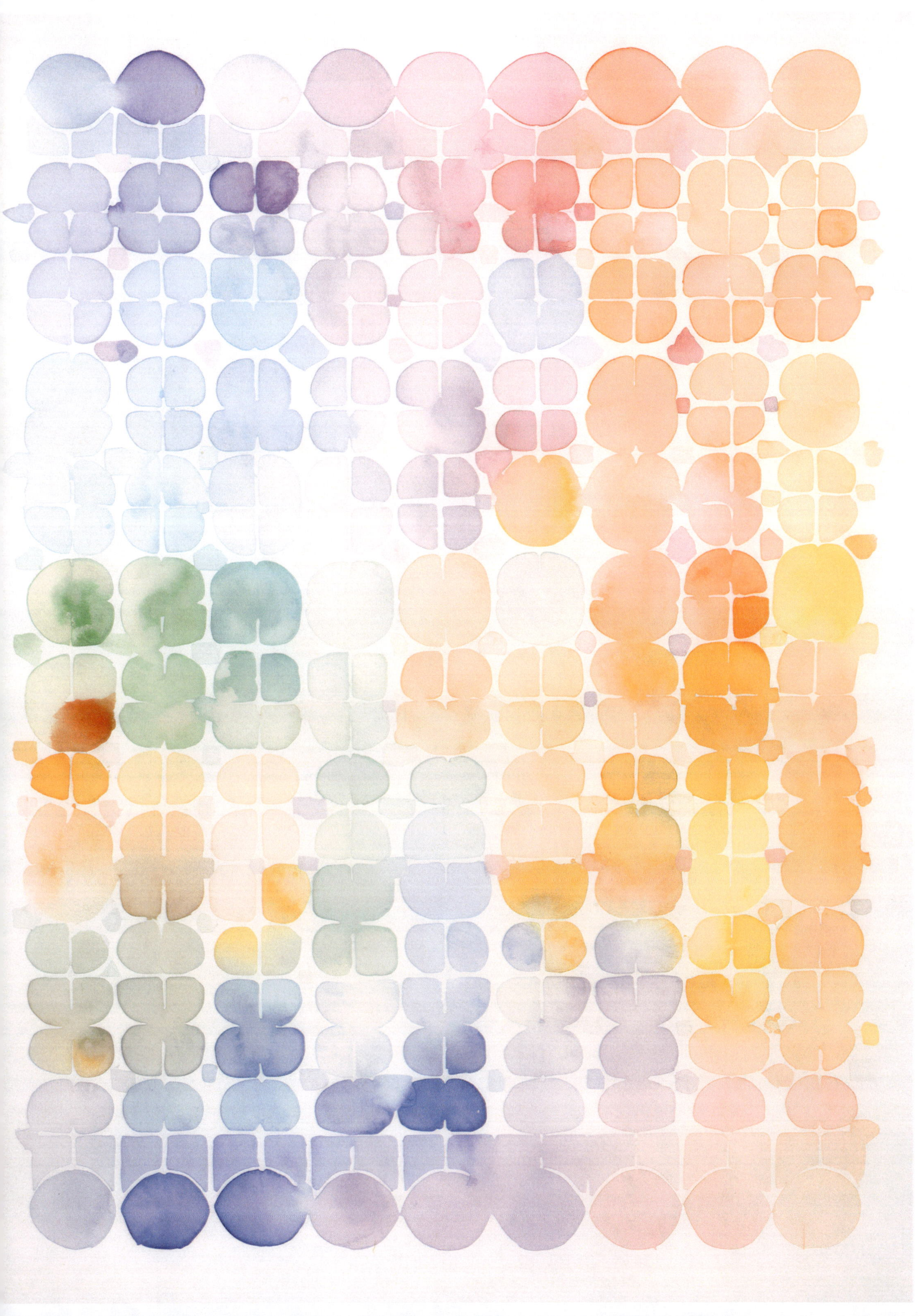

Intentionally left blank

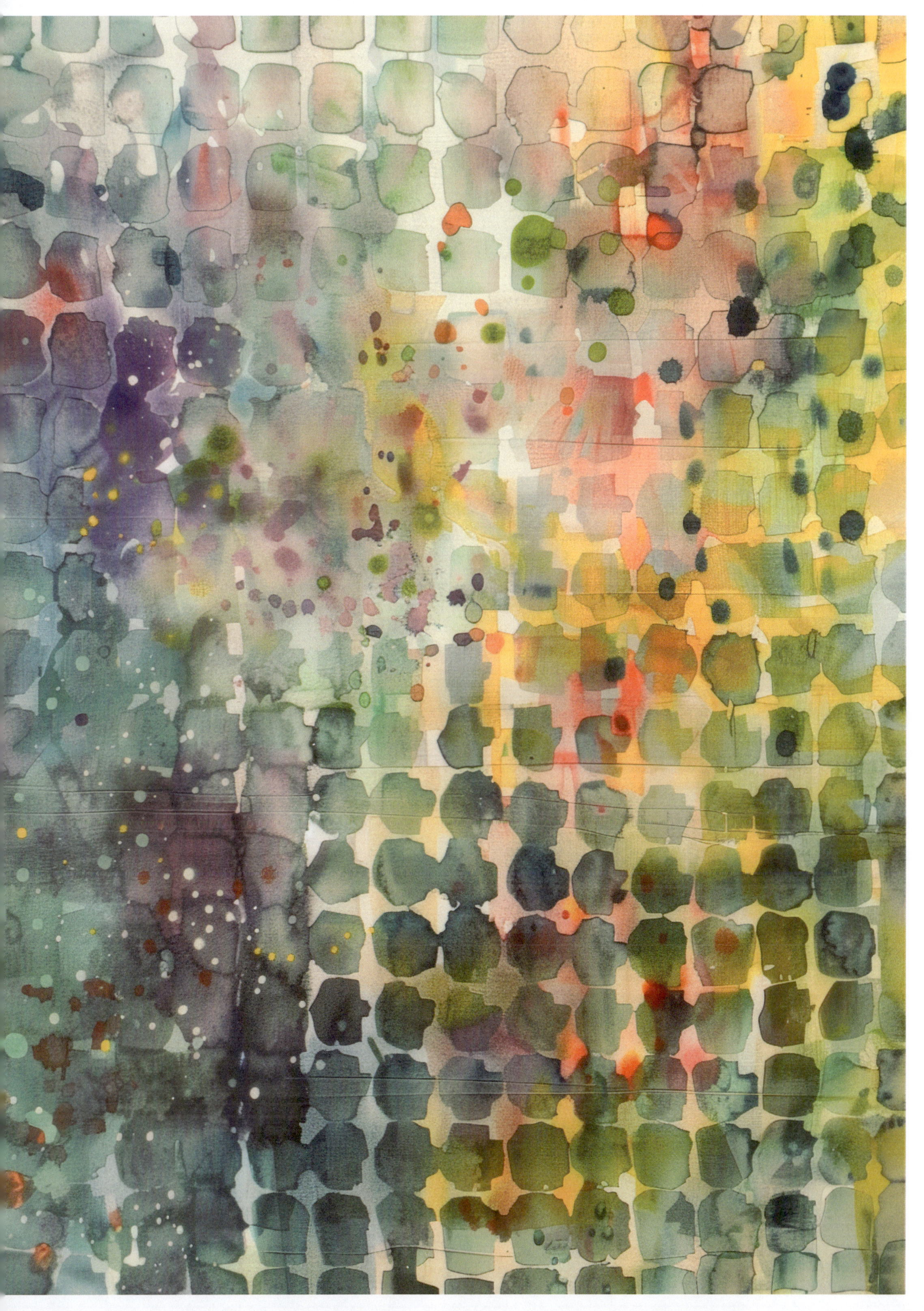

Intentionally left blank

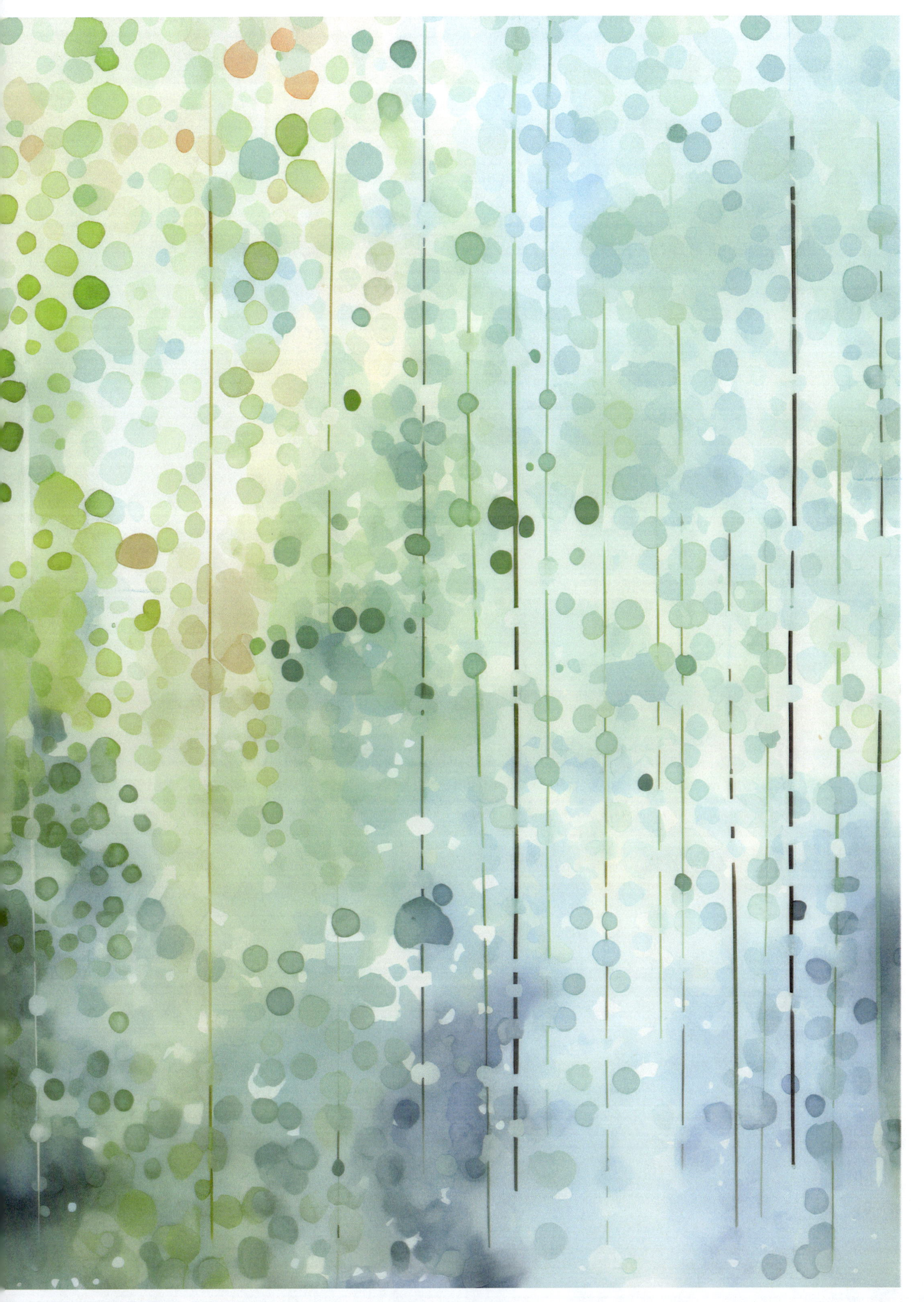

Intentionally left blank

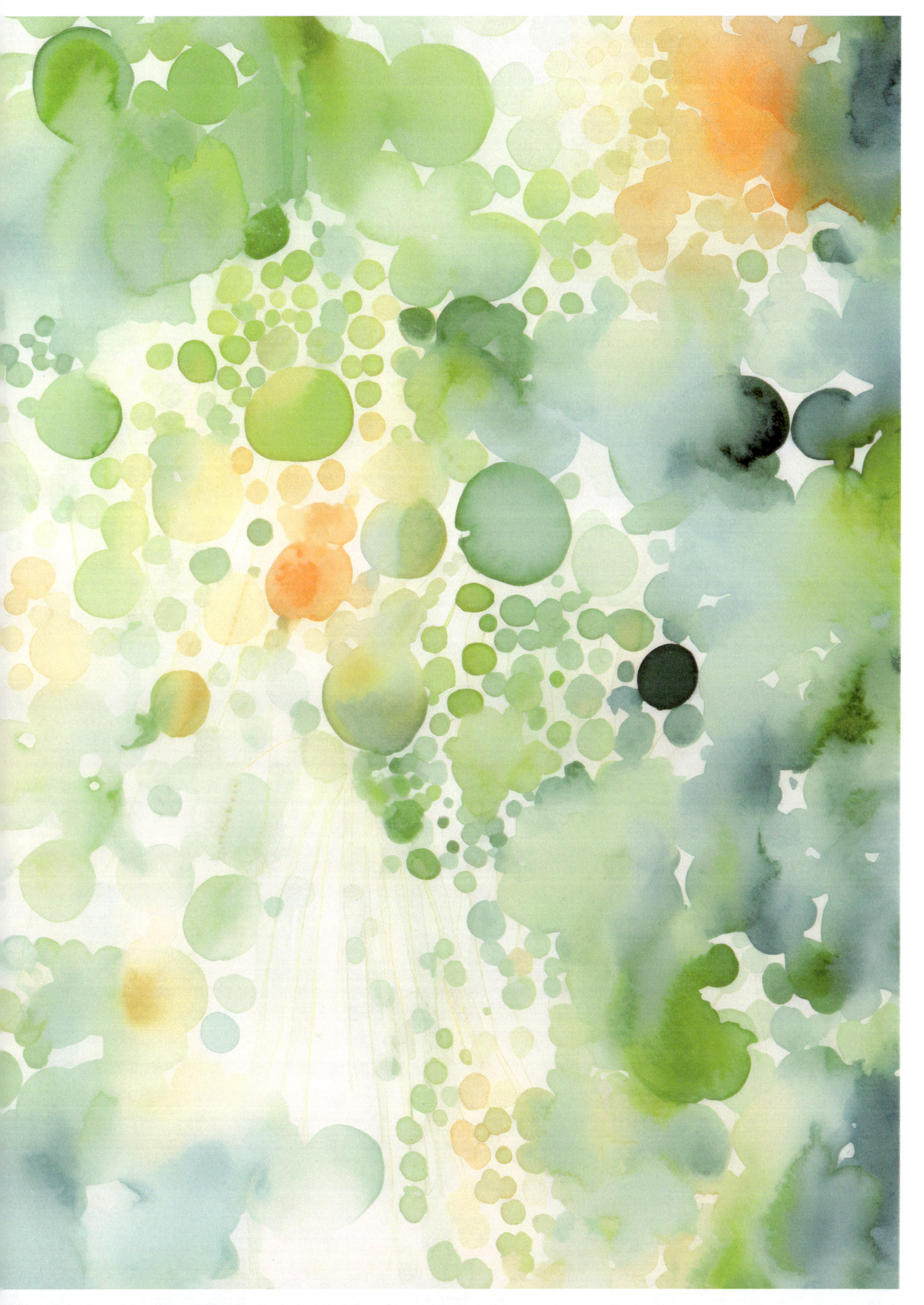

Intentionally left blank

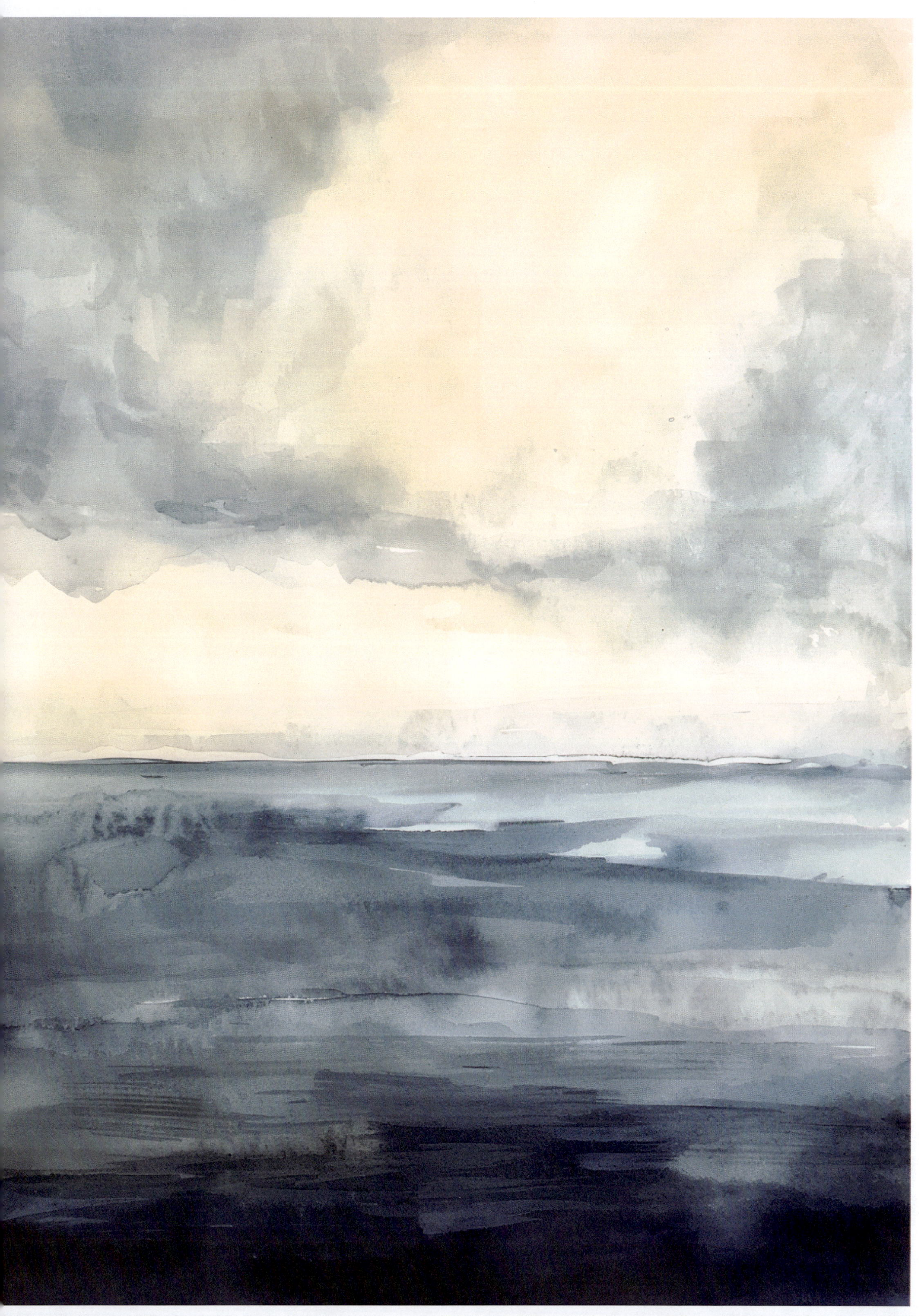

Intentionally left blank

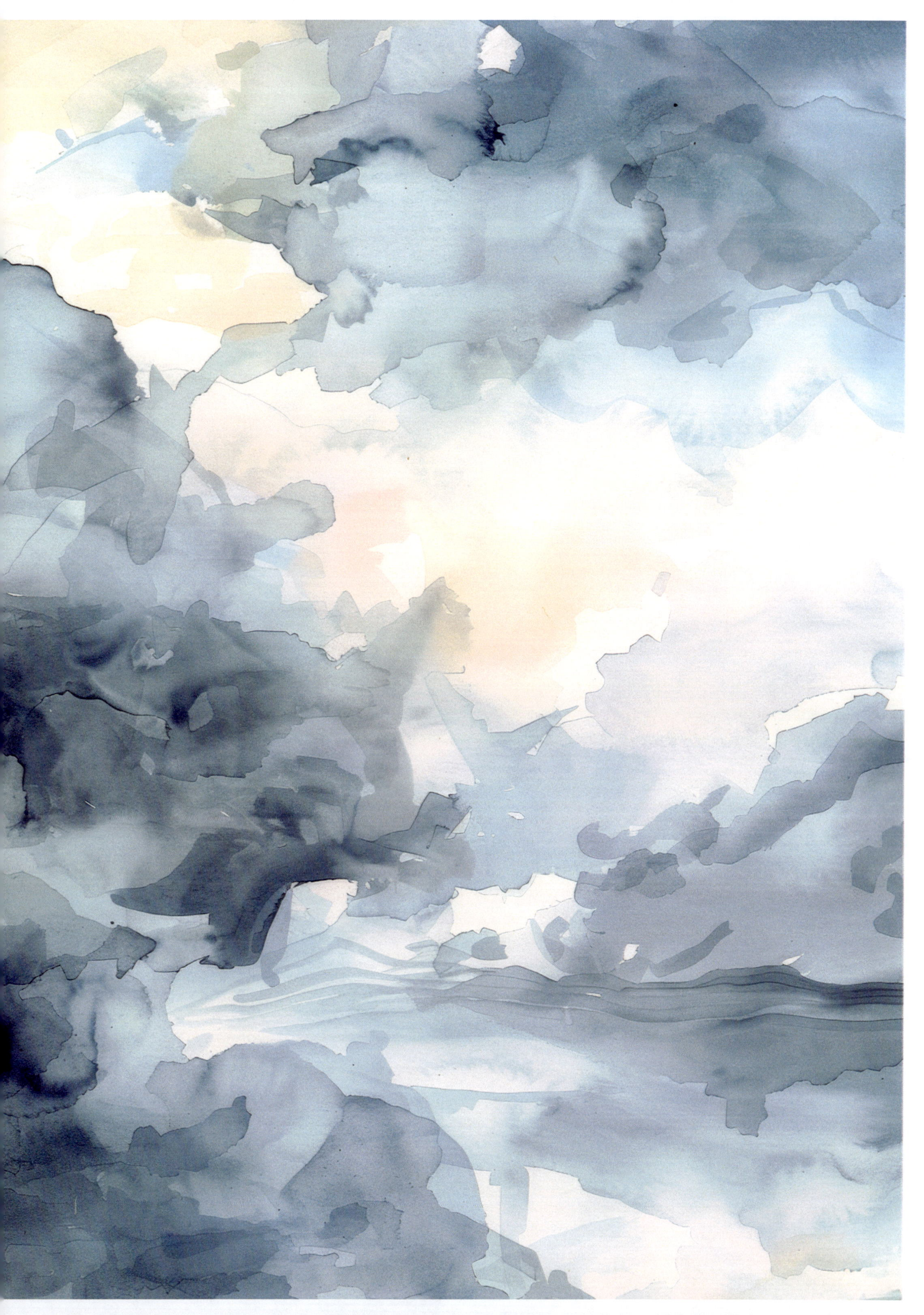

Intentionally left blank

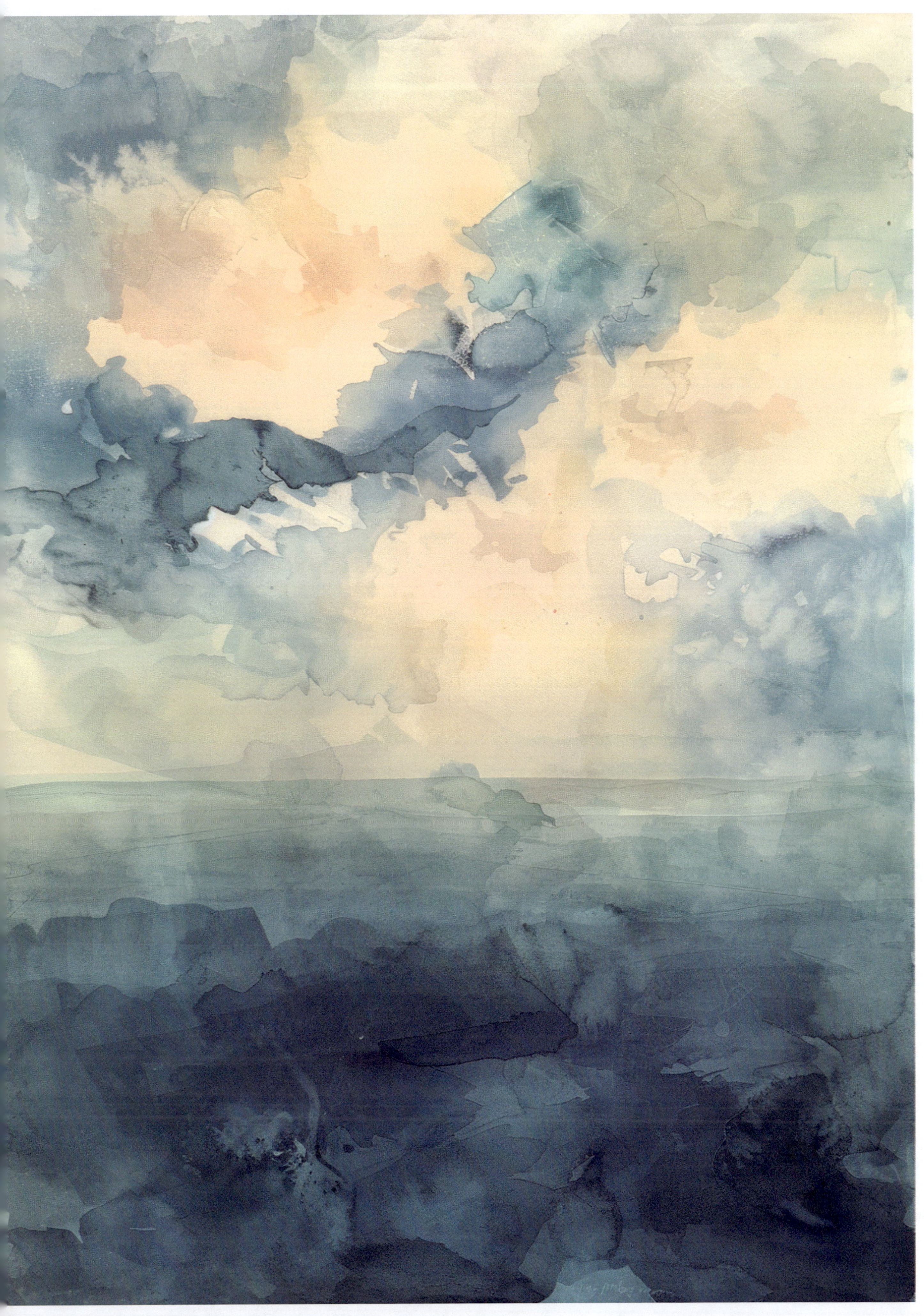

Intentionally left blank

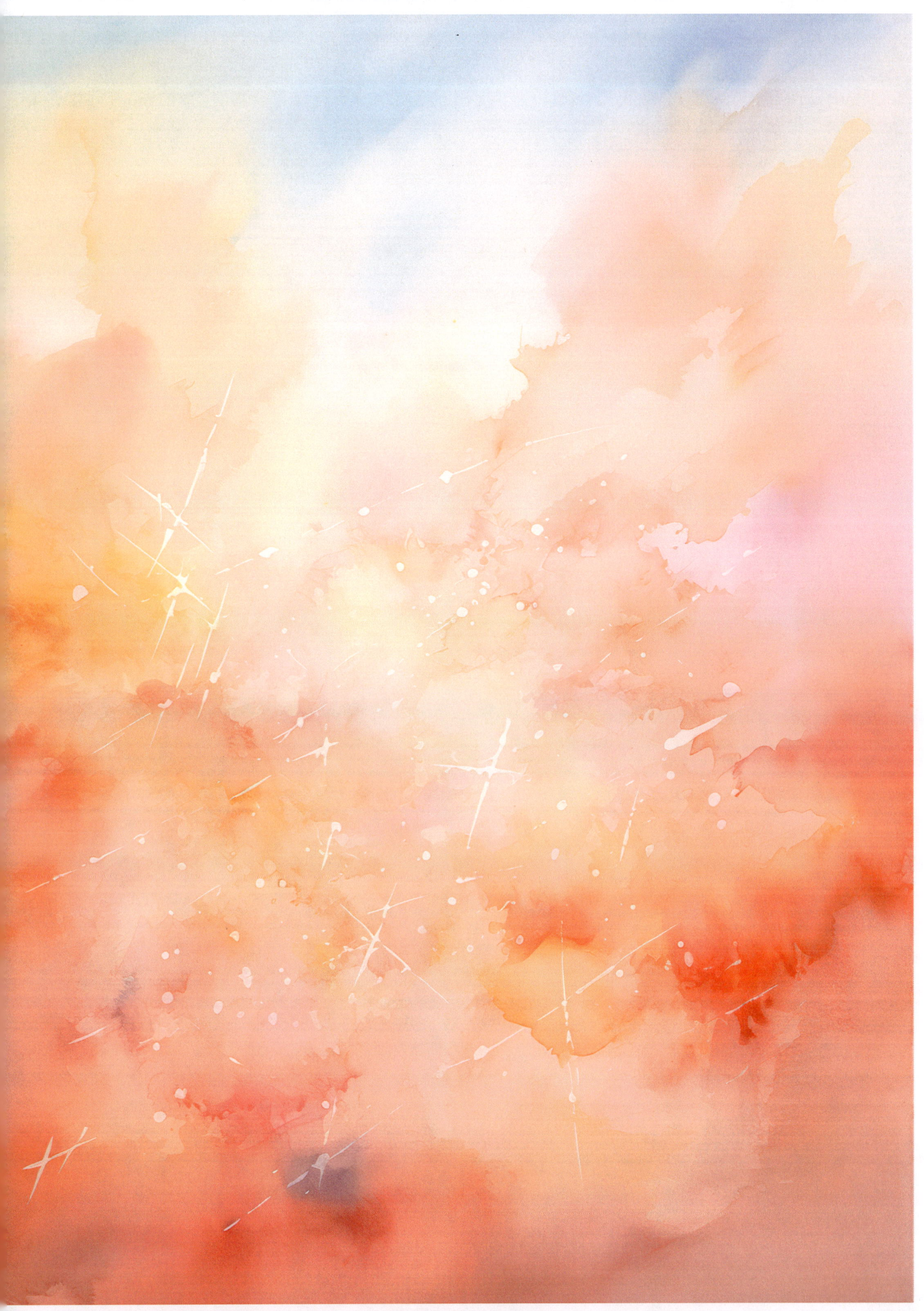

Intentionally left blank

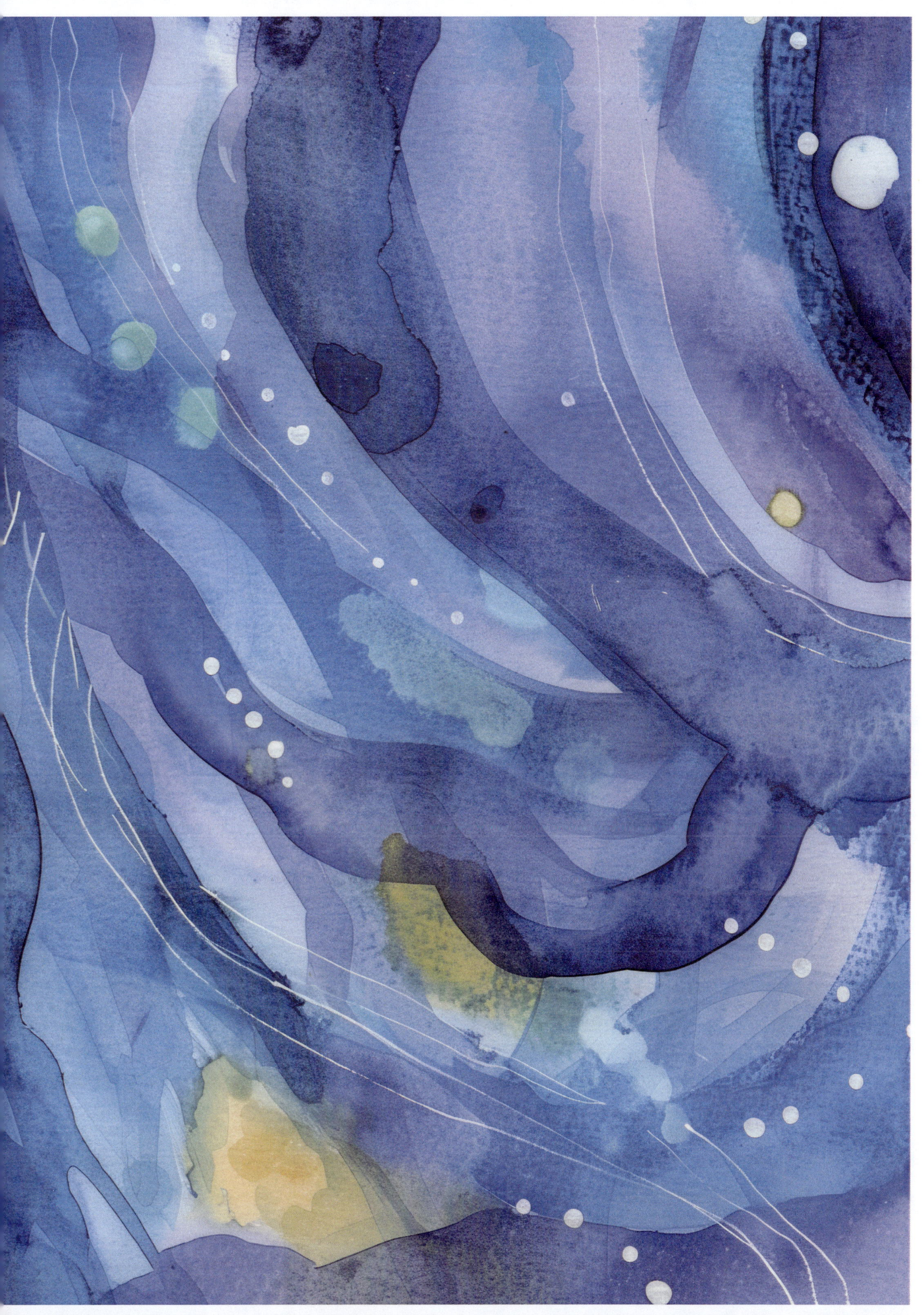

Intentionally left blank

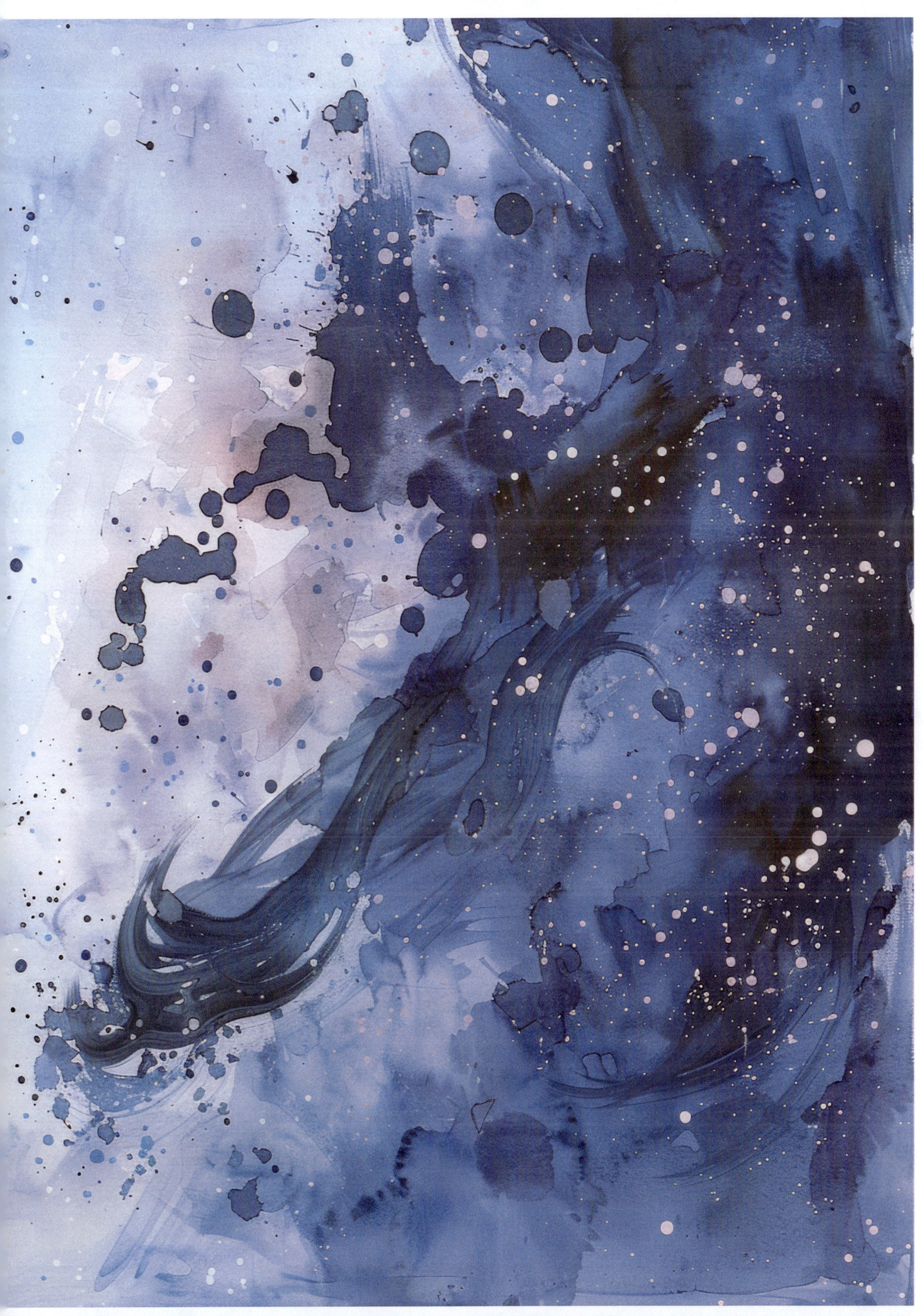

Intentionally left blank

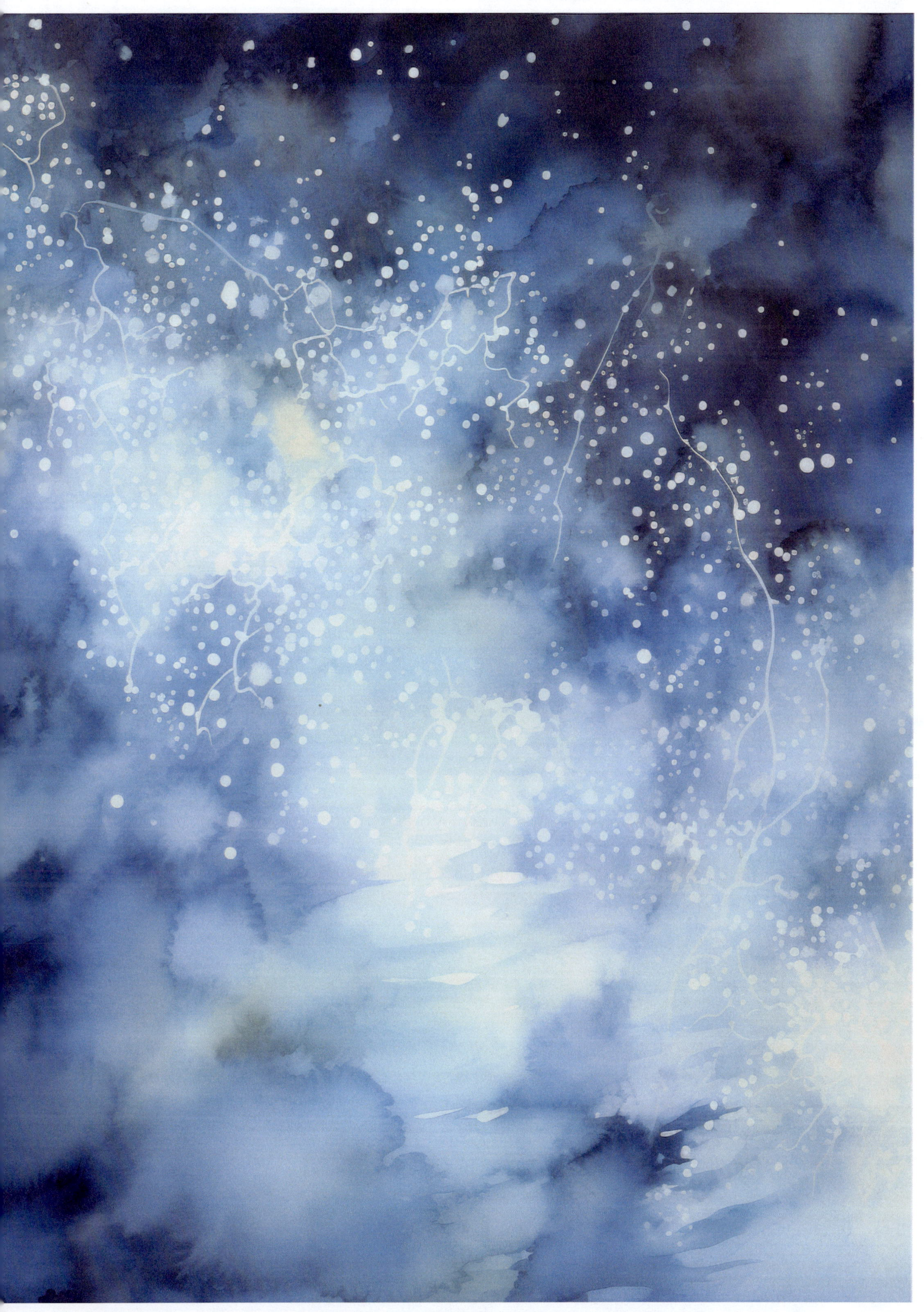

Intentionally left blank

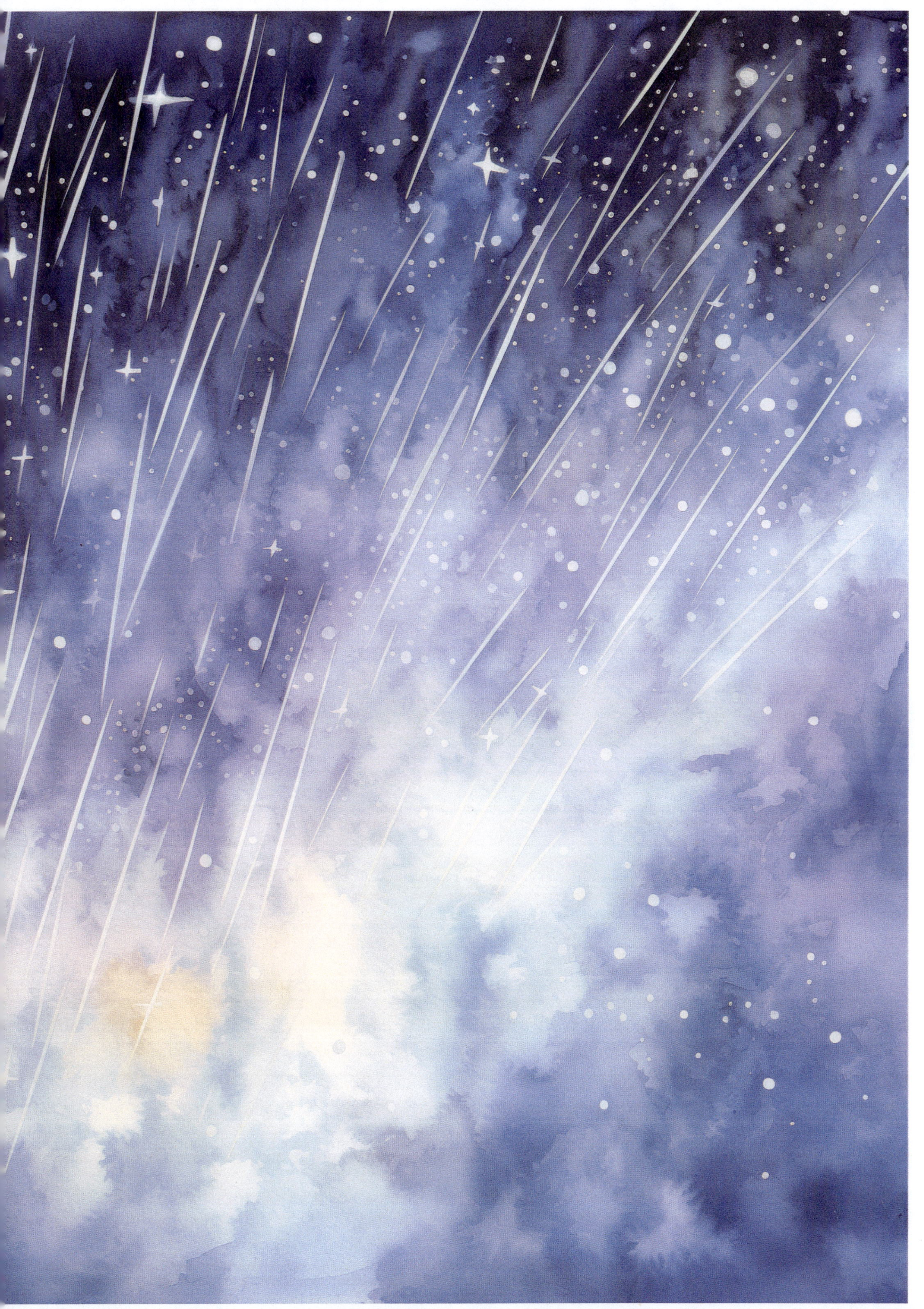

Intentionally left blank

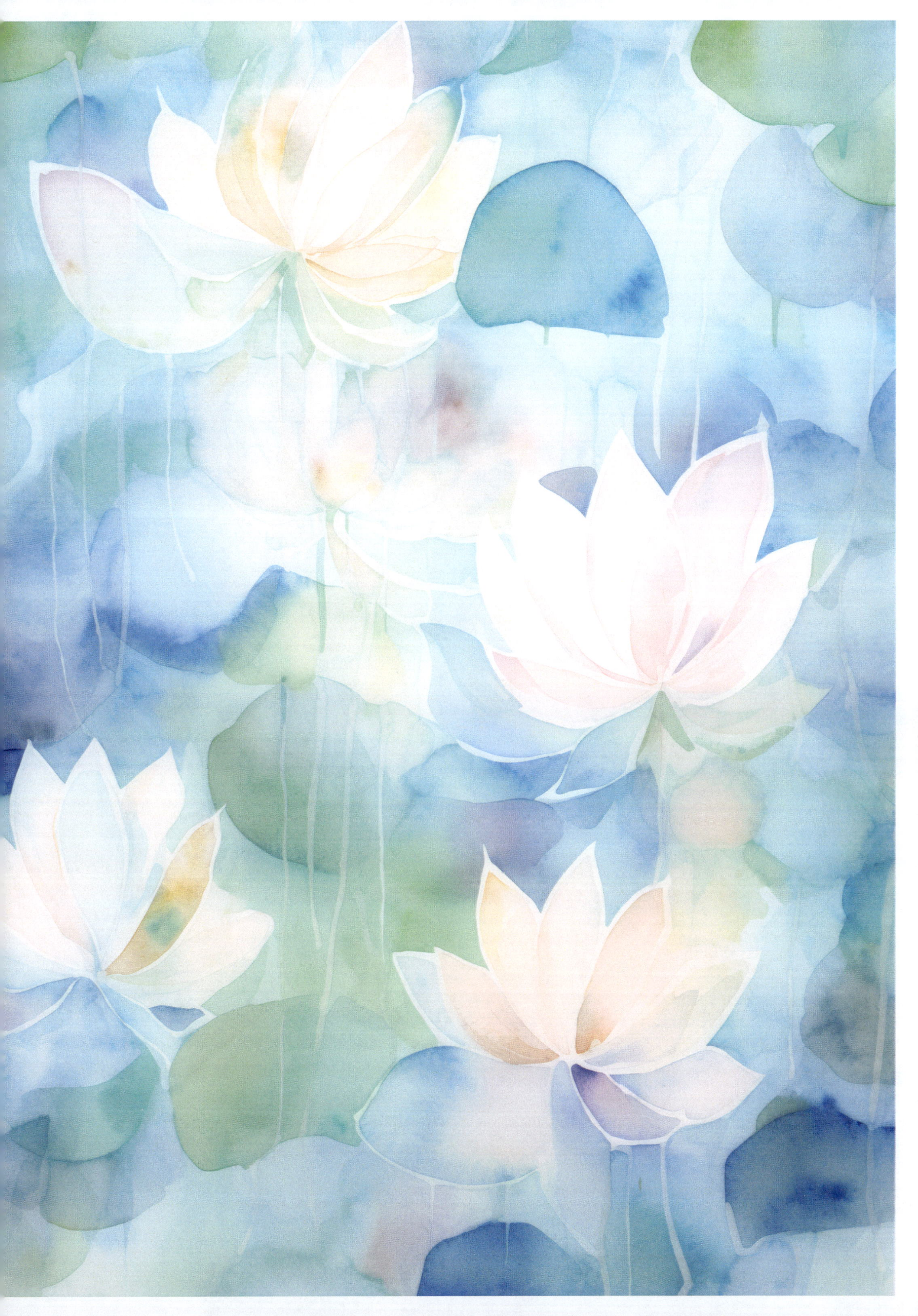

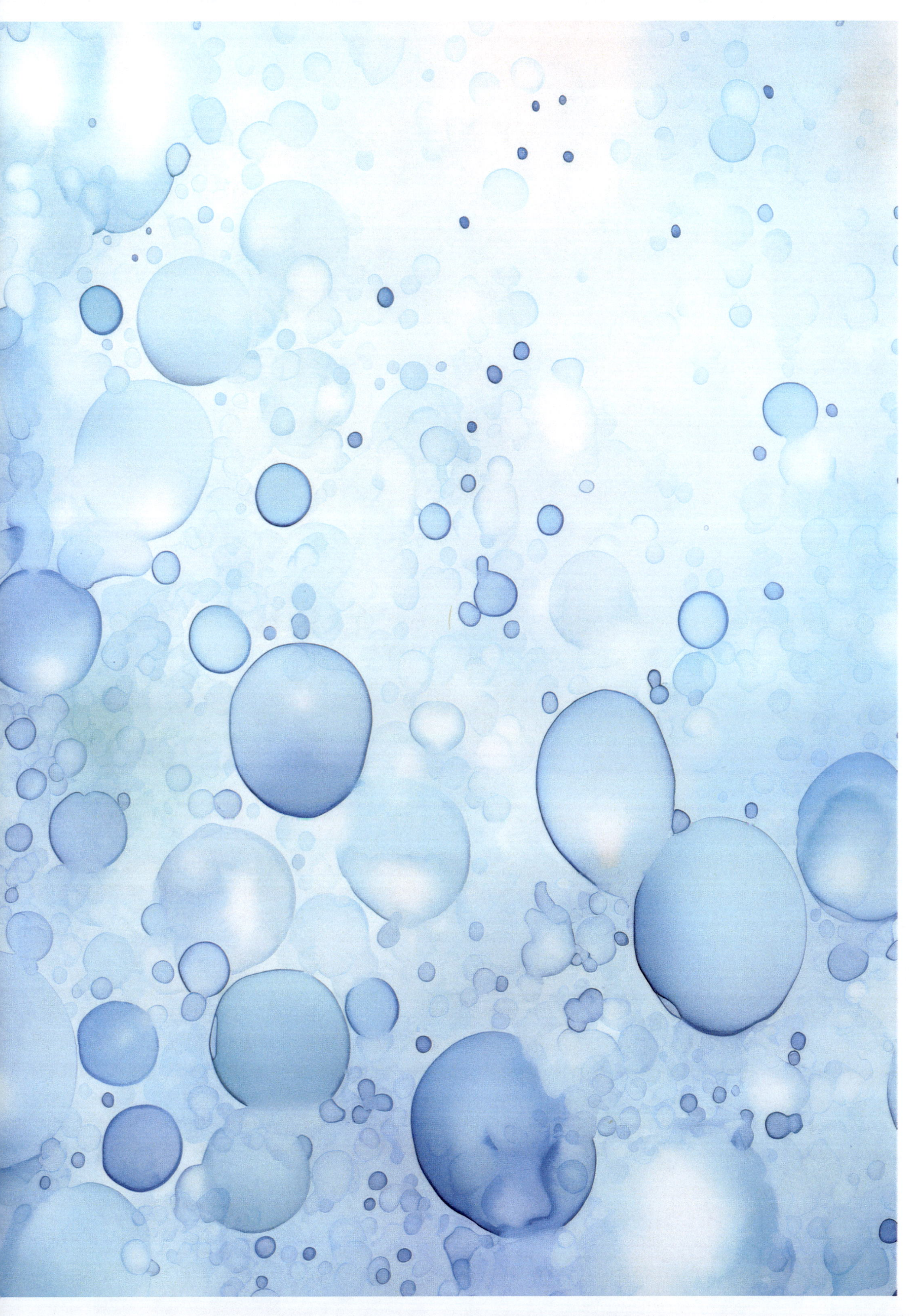

Intentionally left blank

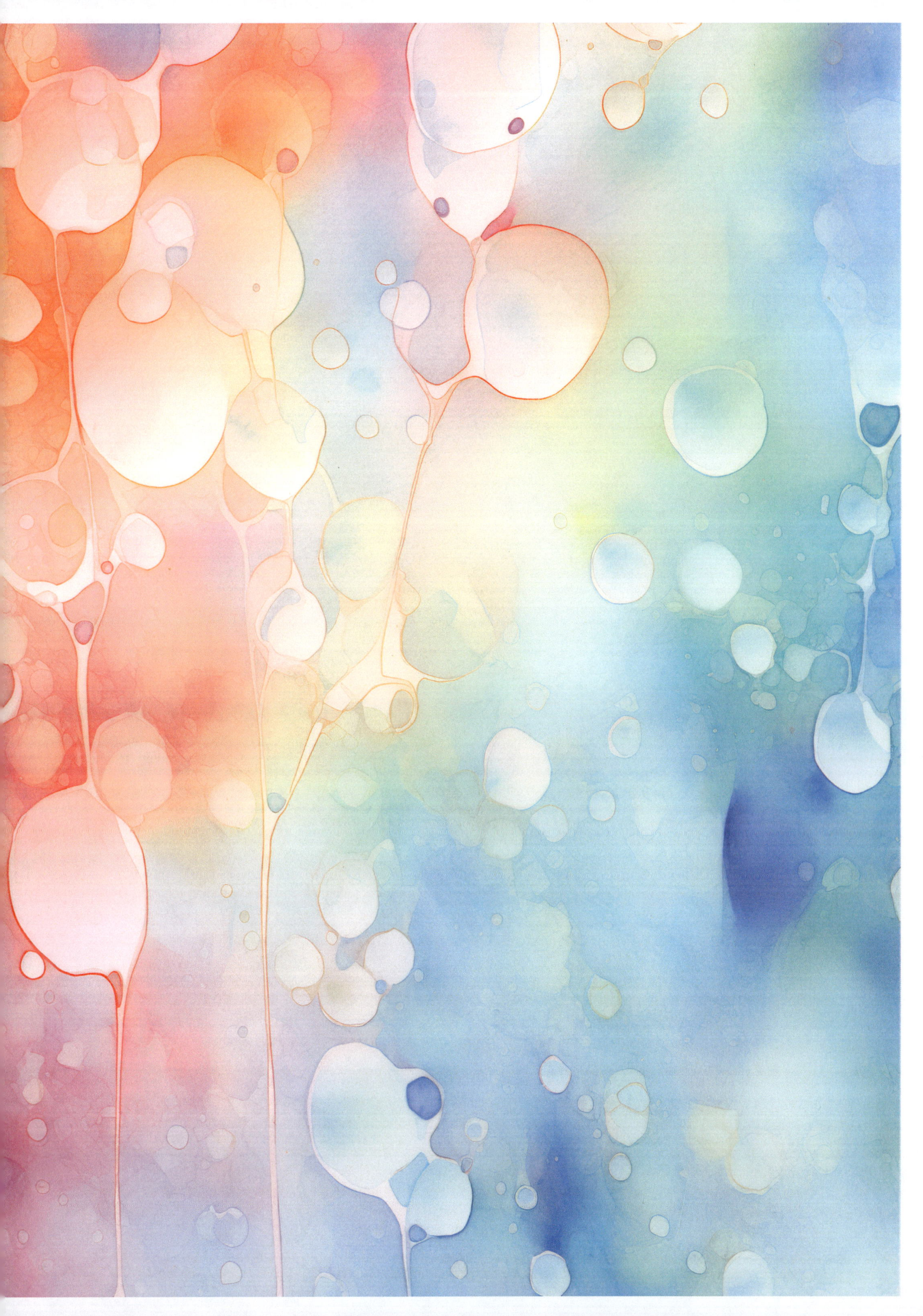

Intentionally left blank

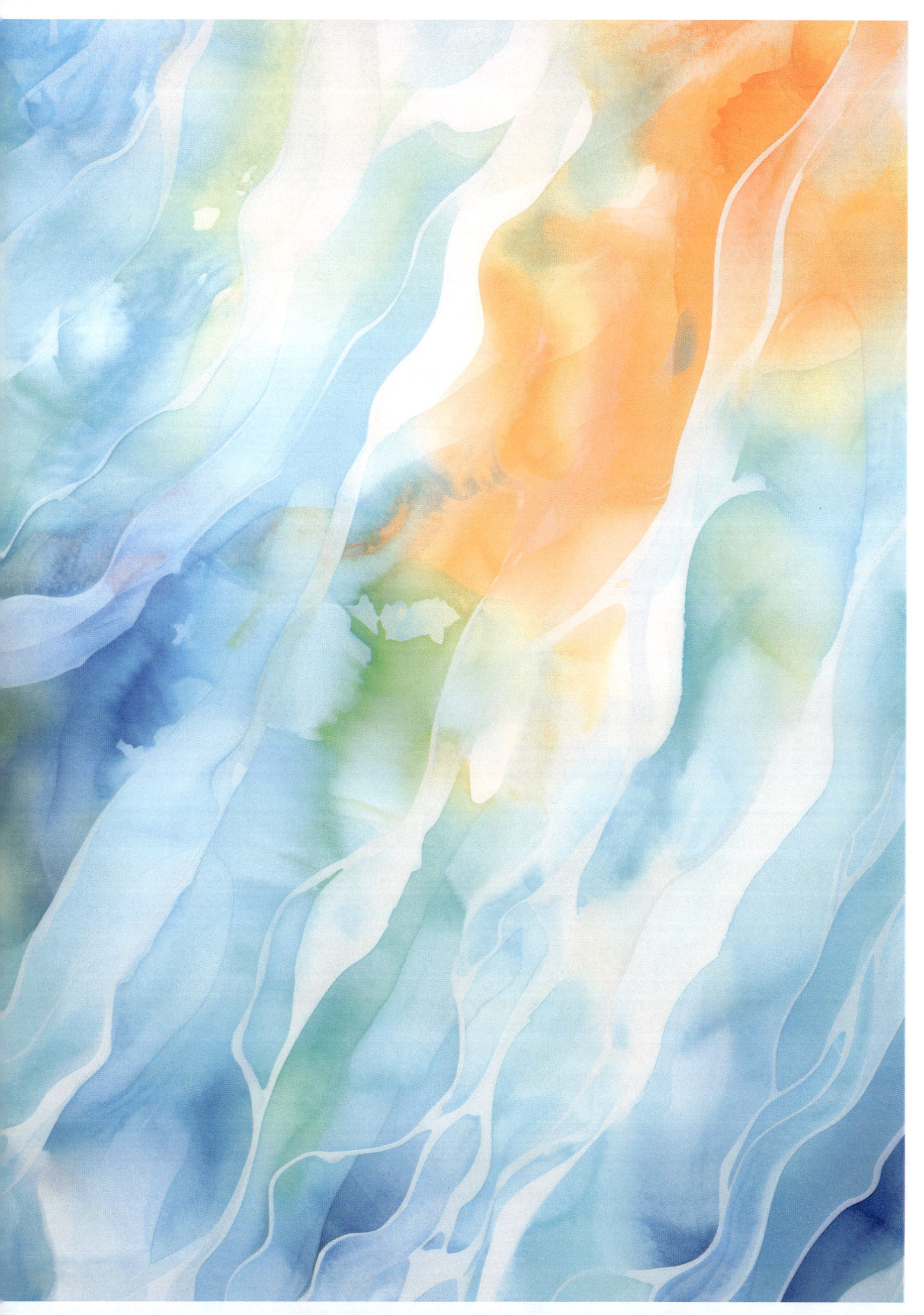

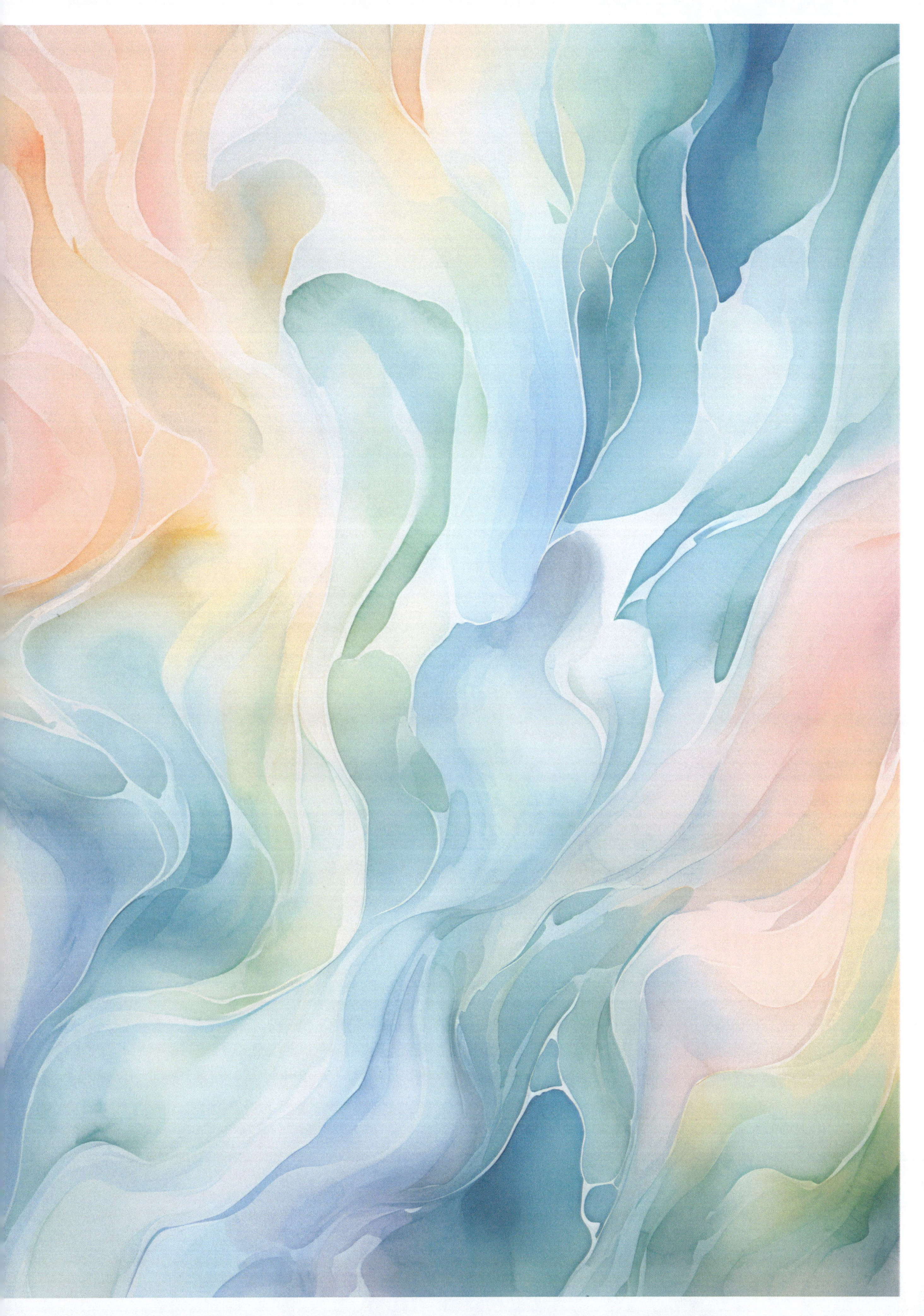

Intentionally left blank

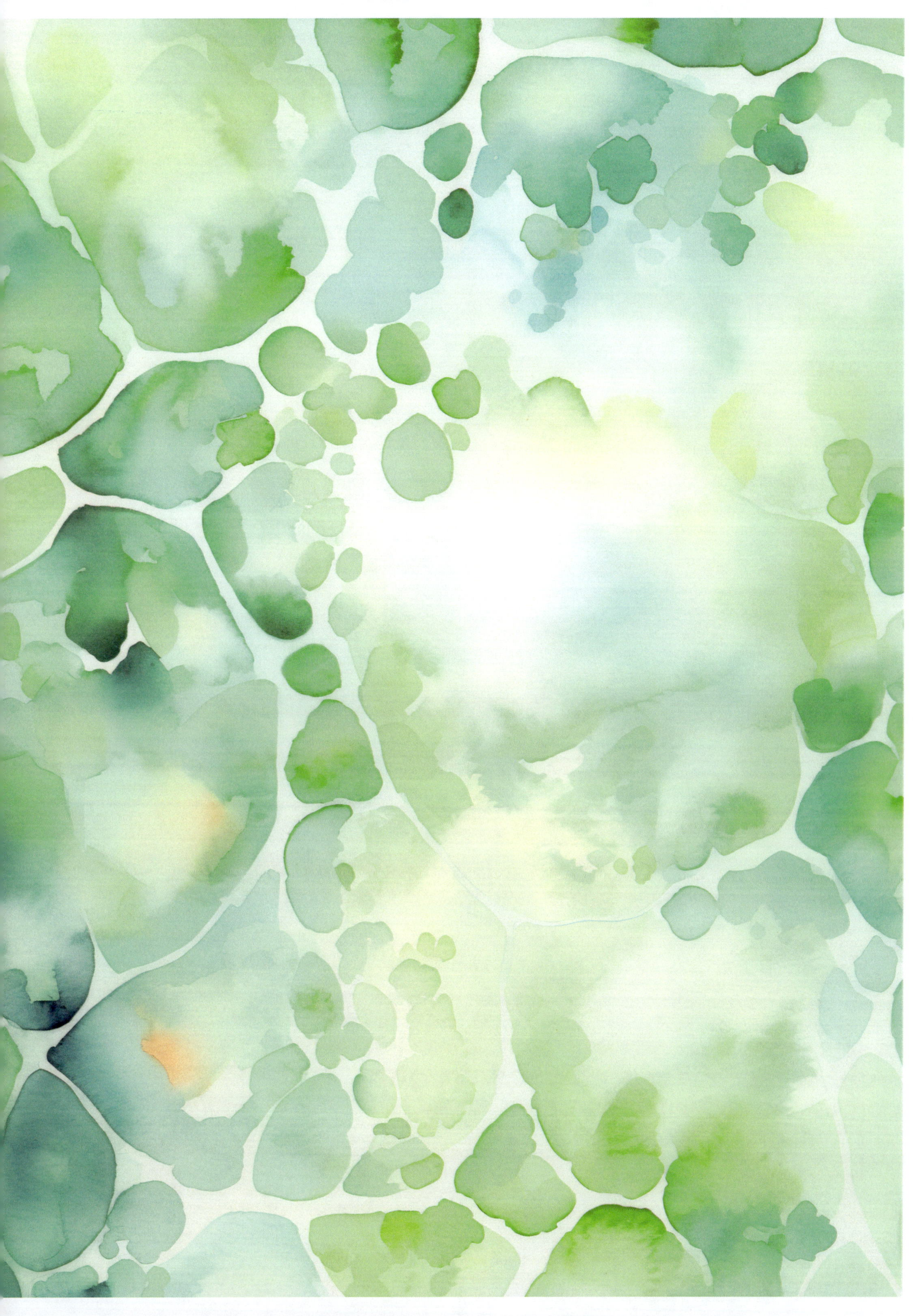

Intentionally left blank

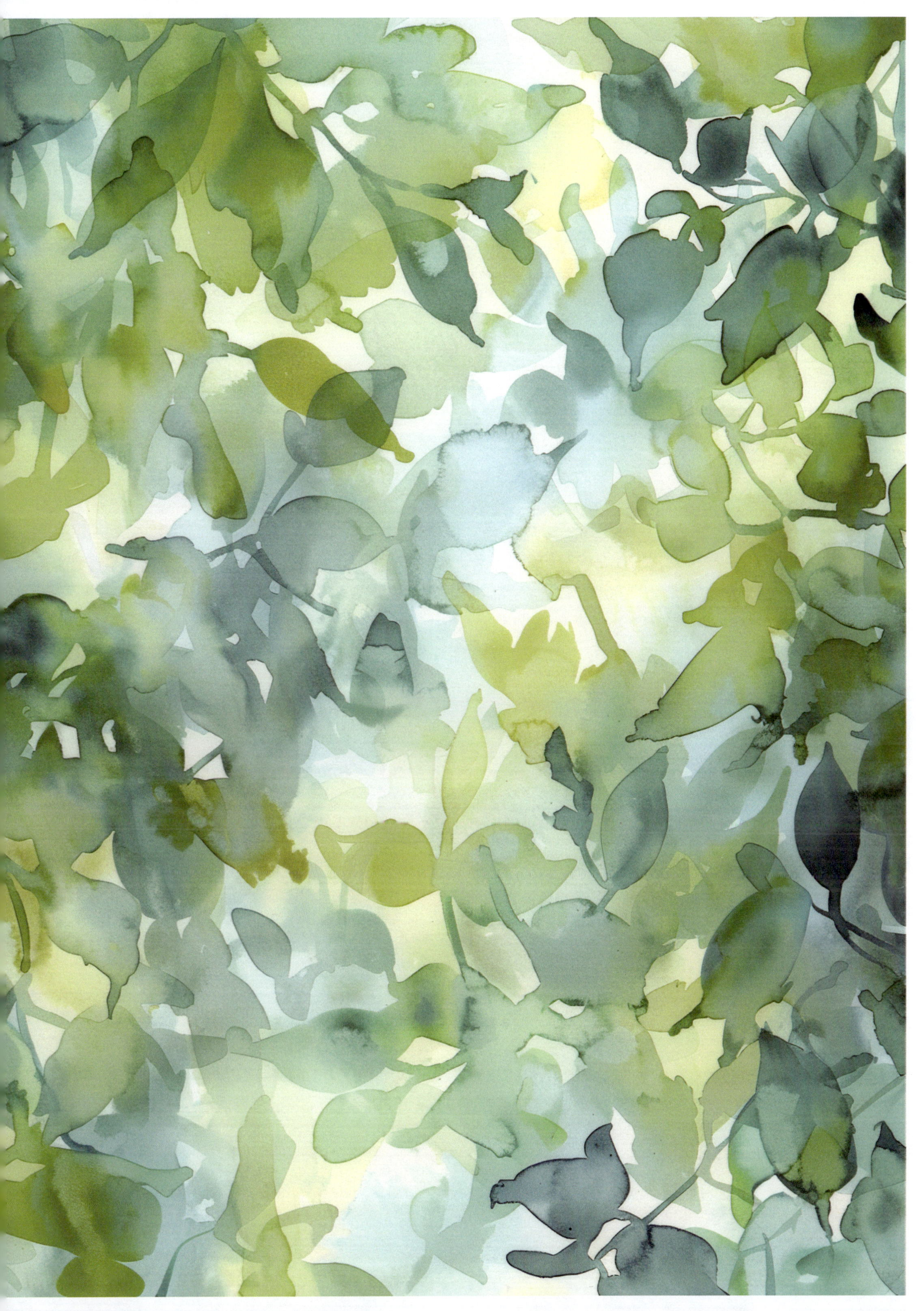

Intentionally left blank

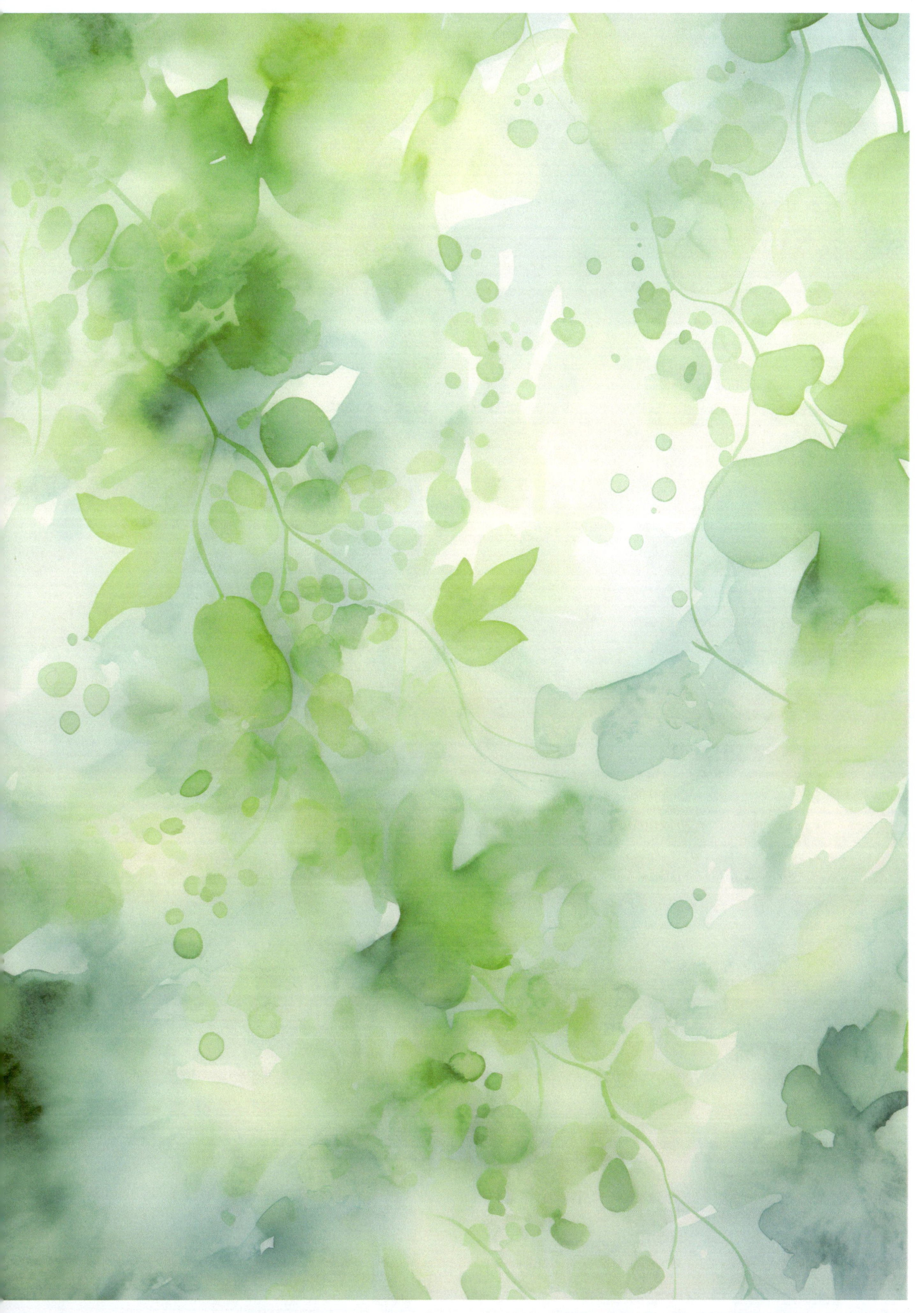

Intentionally left blank

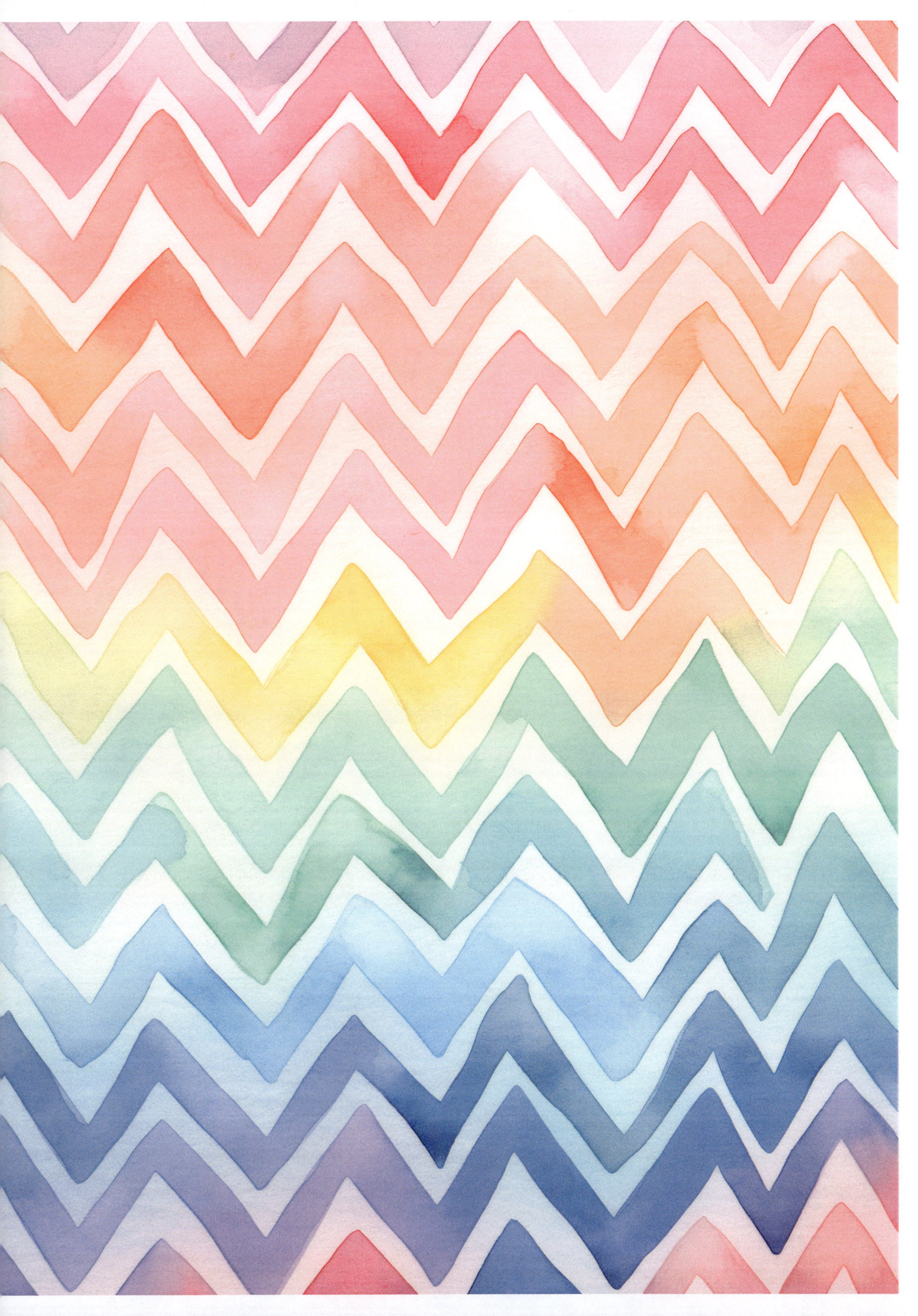

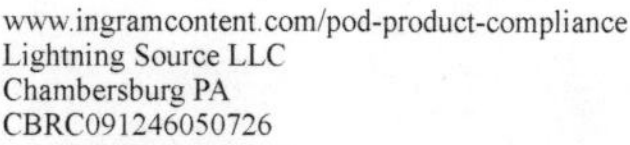